What Can Love Hope For?

What Can Love Hope For?

Questions for Faith Seeking Understanding

William Loader

CASCADE *Books* · Eugene, Oregon

WHAT CAN LOVE HOPE FOR?
Questions for Faith Seeking Understanding

Cascade Books
An Imprint of Wipf and Stock Publishers
199 W. 8th Ave., Suite 3
Eugene, OR 97401

www.wipfandstock.com

HARDCOVER ISBN: 978-1-7252-7080-0

Cataloguing-in-Publication data:

Names: Loader, William.
Title: What can love hope for? : questions for faith seeking understanding / by William Loader.
Description: Eugene, OR: Cascade Books, 2020 | Includes bibliographical references and index.

Subjects: LCSH: Bible. New Testament—Criticism, interpretation, etc. | Faith | Love—Biblical teaching | Christian life
Classification: BS2395 L63 2020 (print) | BS2395 (ebook)

Contents

Preface

When I was a young child my father used to say to me, "Billy, never be afraid to ask questions." I took that to heart and many years later could ground it in an understanding of God as no less generous and encouraging. Explore, inquire, learn, question, and don't feel you have to have answers for everything. It is OK not to know. It is always OK to tell the truth as you see it and it is always wise to listen to others, because you will not always see everything and sometimes you will be unaware of your blind spots.

"What Can Love Hope For?" While this is the title of one of this book's chapters, it is also a recurrent theme throughout the book. The subtitle, "Questions for Faith Seeking Understanding," reflects the fact that this book addresses a number of issues which concern me as a person of faith and as a New Testament scholar as I reflect on the New Testament and the way it has been and is being read and misread today. Some are troubling trends with a long history. Some are already present in the writings of the New Testament itself. Many remain unaddressed and unquestioned, in part to avoid rocking the boat and upsetting treasured assumptions. Left unaddressed, however, they eat away at the integrity and health of our faith and, to return to the maritime metaphor, the calm of not asking questions allows the boat to drift on sometimes in directions which appear well off course from where it all set sail in Jesus.

I dedicate this book, therefore, to all who love their faith and want to take it seriously and engage their minds to embrace it. It is an invitation to reflect on key issues that have shaped Christianity for better and for worse over its existence and brought health and harm to the world. My primary concern is not to promote the answers that make best sense to me but to open up the questions for faith with understanding. This is more than a discussion of ideas. It is faith wanting to be faithful to its calling to be good news in the world and to connect faith to action.

All of the chapters that follow are completely new. I have grouped them under the headings of Faith, Hope, and Love—"Faith: What Can Love Believe?"; "Hope: What Can Love Hope For?"; and "Love: What Can Love Do?" For me faith begins with my understanding of God and that means for me starting with Jesus. So, the first three chapters ask questions about Jesus and God. The second cluster flows on from the first in following up what was the heart of Jesus' message: hope. The final four chapters turn their attention to love, love as the heart of the biblical law and love as replacing biblical law. They look also at serious issues of how the first believers handled rejection, and the strategies, healthy and otherwise, they developed to deal with it and also to promote their message. The final chapter looks at the wide range of matters concerning sex and human relations.

Some of the questions, especially in the section on faith, appear to be rhetorical, expecting the answer, "No". They are, however, more than that because, as I argue, the answer in practice has often been, "Yes." The title I gave to the first draft of this book was "Grit in My Shoe." It reflected the discomfit I sometimes feel as one who both stands in and expounds the Christian tradition. Sometimes it grates with love. I often said to ministry students: you will be bearers of a tradition that has brought health and harm to this world and still does. One of your responsibilities is to discern the difference and be bearers of life not death. That title, "Grit in My Shoe," missed, however, the positive emphases of the book, its exposition of what brings life and health. It is a book about love and reflects a lifetime of engaging with the New Testament text both as a scholar and as a reflective human being committed to self-critical honesty and truth.

As I put the finishing touches to this book, I am aware of being in a world in turmoil over the spread of the COVID-19 coronavirus pandemic. The impact for some is mild but for others is catastrophic, death on a massive scale. The measures required to control its spread are also forcing many into dire straits as economies all but collapse. For many it means isolation and quarantine, for some leading to an acute sense of loneliness and abandonment. The situation is much worse in the so-called two-thirds world of developing countries ill-equipped to deal with the crisis.

In response to the crisis we have seen also some remarkable acts of kindness and generosity: love in the midst of danger and death. Some politicians have awakened from their obsession with marketing themselves and their tribe to recover a humanity rarely seen before. To love and care has taken center stage costing billions, at least in countries able to respond in this way. My hope is that this revival of compassion may last and then continue on to inform whatever normality ensues and be applied worldwide. That, too, is what love can hope for.

I have written this book without references to the scholarly literature which has accompanied me over the past 50 years as a New Testament researcher, not out of ingratitude for the exchange, but to simplify the reading task. At the end of the Afterword I include reference to works in which I engage these issues in scholarly dialogue. If you want to know more of my journey in faith and scholarship before you begin, you may want to start at the end of the book with the Afterword.

I am grateful for all who read and commented on earlier drafts of this book: Ivan Head, Karen Sloan, Betty Stroud, and Nancy Victorin-Vangerud.

Unless otherwise indicated by an asterisk (*) where I use my own translation, quotations from the Bible are from the New Revised Standard Version. All chapters begin with quotations from Scripture, but frequently in an intentionally misconstrued form. Reader beware!

William Loader
Easter, 2020

SECTION A

Faith: What Can Love Believe?

1

Jesus—an Exception in the Life of God?

The Son of Man came not to serve but to be served
and give his life as an example to many.
(with apologies to Mark 10:45)

NOWHERE IS SUCH A reading of Mark 10:45 attested, but, on the other hand, it is widely attested in substance in the lived experience of the church. Did Jesus not come seeking followers who might worship him? Is this not what makes him like God? Or is he different from God or an exception to the way God is? What is God's way?

Did you ever play dressing up? Susan played dressing up and one day she declared: "I'm dressing up as God." Her mother smiled: what next! Into the play clothes cupboard, into the kitchen . . . what would she do? There were crowns and swords, magic wands and angel wings, lots to work with. Mother had to close her eyes and wait. "I'm ready. You can look," Susan cried. And there she was with a simple dress, a bowl of water and a towel. She explained: "I thought God was just like Jesus." She had remembered a story. It said it all.

What does it mean to be great? Doesn't it mean that people will serve you? You will be in charge? Isn't that why we use models for God and Jesus drawn from court rituals where people prostrate themselves before a king? Is it not true that leaders, including leaders in the church, are to be treated in similar ways?

Mark on Greatness

Such questions underlie an issue that the author of the Gospel according to Mark addresses in Mark 8–10. Very different from the subverted version of Mark 10:45 above, the authentic version of the saying attested in the manuscripts reads: "The Son of Man came not to be served but to serve and to give his life a ransom for many" (authentically Mark 10:45).

This statement comes as the climax of Jesus' conflicts with his disciples, which begin back in Mark 8. There Jesus asked them, who people were saying that he was (8:27). Having heard their reports, that people were saying he was John the Baptist or Elijah or one of the prophets, Jesus asked them what they thought. Peter replied: "You are the Christ (the Messiah)" (8:29). He was surely right. Indeed, this is the first occasion where the disciples hail him as the Messiah in Mark's Gospel.

Such a declaration was, however, dangerous. Thus, Jesus tells them not to tell anyone (8:30). It was dangerous because many people expected the Messiah to be someone who would lead the nation to freedom, defeat their enemies, and as king of the Jews, successfully establish God's kingdom. It was revolutionary and to announce that Jesus was the Messiah publicly would put him in danger. The Roman authorities had no tolerance for subversive movements and their would-be Messiahs, whether they planned their battles by force of arms or by force of ideas. Indeed, they would crucify Jesus, when the secret got out, to deter such aspirations, mounting the charge over him as "King of the Jews."

Jesus adds to his warning in 8:30 the statement that he would face suffering and rejection by the authorities, and would be executed, before rising from the dead (8:31). This upsets Peter whose understanding of messiahship was that Jesus would be triumphant and successful, as most people expected a Messiah to be. Peter even starts to challenge Jesus and the exchange becomes quite sharp (8:32–33). Jesus calls him Satan and declares that he has his mind on human values not on God's values. This will have puzzled Peter, because for him to be on God's side was to be on the winning side. Jesus and Peter had very different ideas about God and God's ways.

Next, Jesus gives the disciples instructions about what it means to follow him (8:34–37). It means not to make oneself the center of everything, but to give up selfish ambition and even be prepared to take up the cross. The human values for which Peter was advocating meant trying to be a winner. Jesus puts it in terms typical of his confronting style: What does it

4

profit a person if they gain the whole world and lose their soul, their real being?

For Peter to be on God's side meant to win and to gain power and wealth—to be great, a common human foible. Jesus advocated a very different understanding of greatness and what is profitable. Greatness in Jesus' understanding is not making oneself the center of attention to be served and true profit is not gaining wealth and power, but rather it is being prepared to be lowly and loving, to serve others. That was his way and that was to be the way of his disciples.

In the next chapter we again find Jesus confronting his disciples. Again, he repeats that he is on a road that will bring suffering and death (9:31), but he learns that they had been arguing about who among them was the greatest (9:33–34). He subverts their values with the statement: "If anyone wants to be first, he will need to be last and servant of all" (9:35). Then he takes a little child, weak and vulnerable, as his model. The assumption is that the little child has not yet learned to try to play the games of power. That is the way Jesus is and that is the way they are to be. Can they accept and value such a little child and value being like a little child? Then they could accept and value Jesus and indeed, God, because neither of them plays the power game.

A third time we find the disciples in conflict with Jesus. This comes in Mark 10 where James and John approach Jesus wanting the top two positions of power in what they hoped would be Jesus' victorious kingdom as the Messiah (10:35–40), despite his repeating for a third time that his path would lead him to suffering and death (10:33–34). They have failed to understand Jesus' teaching and what it means to follow him. Their approach annoys the other disciples (10:41), probably because they might have wanted such power, too.

Jesus' response to the disciples expands his teaching (10:40–45). He points to the way rulers of this world like to have power and dominate people. They see that as their greatness. Again, he repeats his message: if you want to be great, you need to learn to be a servant, a carer. In very confronting language he subverts normal values, declaring that to be truly great is even to be a slave. It is then that he brings the statement with which our discussion began: "For the Son of Man came not to be served but to serve and to give his life a ransom for many" (10:45).

While Mark brings this teaching especially in Mark 8–10, he continues it in the story of Jesus' last days in Jerusalem and his crucifixion. He truly is the Messiah, the "King of the Jews," but a very different kind of Messiah. His throne is a cross. His crown is a crown of thorns. Love and lowliness even to the point of death are the way of Jesus and according to his teaching this is true greatness and also how the disciples should understand themselves.

These are what he declares are also God's values, which Peter failed to see, leading to Jesus' rebuke: "Get behind me, Satan! For you are setting your mind not on God's priorities but on human priorities" (8:33). This then becomes difficult. Is God like Jesus in this regard? Or is God different?

Jesus and Models of God

Jesus pointed to human models of greatness as represented by rulers and kings (10:42). Popular understandings of God with a long history have pictured God as at least like great human beings, such as rulers and kings, and concluded that God is the king, the ruler of the universe and God's greatness is God's power and might, like that of a great king. Isn't God more like what the disciples understand as great?

Such images of God do, indeed, reflect the disciples' notion of greatness. Indeed, taken to an extreme this notion can lead to images of God as not loving and generous but rather as primarily wanting to be treated like earth's kings: glorified, worshiped, praised, for his own sake. At times God is pictured as being very self-obsessed, wanting the universe to revolve around himself (pictured as male), just like people who want to be self-important.

If God is really like that, then we would have to imagine that Jesus was teaching that there is a big difference between him and God and certainly between us and God. Imagined in this way, we would have to think that God demands that both Jesus and his disciples as loyal subjects must be obedient. That would mean that they must not try to be powerful and great like God, but do the opposite: be kind and loving—because that is what God demands. They are not to be like God at all.

This is not, however, how Jesus talks about God. He speaks of God as king, but a very different kind of king. The kingdom or reign of God is about love and generosity. Jesus did not see himself as an exception to the way God is, but as in touch with and expressing God's being. Jesus was not an exception in the life of God. Rather Jesus reveals what God is like.

When in the parable of the prodigal son Jesus talks about a father running down the road to welcome back a son who had messed up his life, he was talking about himself, but he was also talking about God. Rather than seeing God as like the rulers and kings of this world—self-centered, and great in Peter's sense—Jesus shows us God as generous and caring and using his might and power to that end. Peter's understanding of greatness, including, by implication, God's greatness, is all too human in the worst sense. Jesus' image of God reflecting the best of Jewish tradition is also human or humane, but in the best sense. Love is his model.

Just as faith must subvert popular notions of God's greatness based on all too human models of greatness, so faith needs to subvert popular notions of worship that are based on such models. True worship is, therefore, not the admiration of power. It is awe before the one who is almighty but who uses power to create and redeem. God is not a self-obsessed ruler, nor like a two-year old bent on attention (with apologies to all two-year olds who are not!). God is loving and generous, confronting our models of greatness with the subversiveness of Jesus.

Easter Fulfilling Peter's Dream?

This can all come undone, however, when we think about Easter, especially if we interpret the resurrection as Jesus finally fulfilling Peter's dreams of achieving greatness and glory and leaving love and lowliness behind. Where human notions of God's greatness follow Peter's model, then resurrection comes to be seen as a reversal of what Jesus was. His love and lowliness would then be just a passing phase. Now everything is back to normal. Jesus is enthroned—just like the great kings and rulers of this world, but in the heavenly realm. All he stood for is undone or rendered little more than a stunt or an interim phase. Peter and the disciples were right after all. Only their timing was wrong.

Easter, however, is not to be seen as God saying "no" to Jesus, but as God saying "yes" to Jesus. Rather than now distancing from Jesus' model, God affirms it and him. When we see it this way we understand the resurrection as an act of vindication. God says "yes" to all that Jesus was, what he taught and embodied. His life was not an exception in the life of God, but expressed God's heart. He was and is the Word, the revelation of who God was and is. Indeed, faith celebrates Jesus as the Son, as God incarnate.

It is very troubling that over the centuries the view of the disciples, as Mark portrays it, has been so influential. To hail God in their terms is, in turn, to reinforce the values that having power and wealth is justified and is what makes for greatness. Worship, framed in this way, can subvert the gospel of Jesus, turning him into a model for the pursuit of human greatness. Indeed, it is as though Mark wrote: "The Son of Man did not come to serve but to be served and to give his life as an example for many." Many have followed that example.

Paul's Model of God

Paul understood this well. He spoke of what in human terms appeared to be God's foolishness and weakness and declared that it is true wisdom and strength (1 Cor 1:18–25). "For God's foolishness is wiser than human wisdom, and God's weakness is stronger than human strength" (1:25). It is especially Paul who unpacks why this subversive message of God as loving works. For it is in opening ourselves to God's generosity, to forgiveness and acceptance, that we become free from preoccupation with ourselves and with concern with our own status. We are able then to have space and energy to respond to others in love, to love our neighbors as and because we love ourselves. Love creates love.

Paul talks of this as the work of the Spirit, first bringing to us the love that sets us right with God and with ourselves, and then producing through us the fruits of the Spirit, especially love: "The fruit of the Spirit is love, joy, peace, patience, kindness, generosity, faithfulness, gentleness, and self-control" (Gal 5:22). Paul celebrates this love in his famous chapter on love in 1 Corinthians 13.

The traditions of the church have been so shaped by models of greatness drawn from the practices and values of royal courts, that it is a constant challenge to hold onto the subversive teaching of Jesus. The disciples so easily win. Many of the songs and hymns we sing appear to side with the disciples.

What is greatness? Paul would answer: love. Where do we see true spirituality, the true marks of the Spirit? In love. Why is this so? Because God is love. Can we still speak of God in royal terms as king? Yes, if we remember that God is the king of love. Are acts and words of worship and adoration appropriate in relation to God? Yes, if our awe responds to God's being as all loving and not as a god who is the projection of human obsession with power and self-centeredness.

> "For the Son of Man came not to be served but to serve and to give his life a ransom for many." (Mark 10:45)

For Reflection: What does this mean for the way we worship? What message do our hymns, songs, prayers convey?

2

Did the Cross Change God's Mind?

There was a man who had two sons. The younger said to his father, "Father, give me the share of the property that will belong to me." So he divided his property between them. A few days later the younger son gathered all he had and travelled to a distant country, and there he wasted his money in wild living. Reaching rock bottom, he decided to return back home. His father saw him coming a long way off and said to himself. "Here's that son who has brought shame on me and my household. There's no way he's coming back here." And he said to his slaves: "Shut the door! Don't let him in!"

Meanwhile the elder brother was coming in from the fields and heard his father's anger and said. "But, dad, he is my brother. He was all but dead and now he wants to come back to life again." So, he went off to the bank, collected his livelihood and said to his father: "Father, look, here is my livelihood. Take it and I will promise to work for three days in the pigsty, if only you will let him in." The father paced up and down and then turned to his son and said: "You are being very generous. OK. It's a deal. And we'd better do the right thing and have a welcoming feast. Make the arrangements and you can butcher that calf." And it was so. (with apologies to Luke 15:11–32)

SUCH A PARABLE IS nowhere attested, but the thoughts that underlie it are widespread and well-attested in communities of Christian faith. Did the cross persuade God to act out of character? Did it change God's mind? Did Jesus' death make forgiveness and salvation possible for the first time? Did

Jesus and God have different values? Was Jesus not like God? What was and is God really like?

As we saw in the previous chapter, for Christian faith Jesus is not an exception in the life of God—on the contrary. How then can it have happened that we have claims that imply Jesus changed God's mind by dying on the cross? The claims take many forms. He took the punishment due to sinners? He paid the penalty for their sins? He satisfied God's offended dignity? He enabled God to make an exception and be loving and forgiving? And only in and since the cross has forgiveness become possible? There are indeed texts in the New Testament that can be used to answer all these questions with: "yes." How has this come about?

The real parable of the Prodigal Son has an opposite message. It is about a parent who cannot give up love for his child, indeed, even before he knows whether the son in coming back is sorry or not. Jesus told this parable to defend the generosity with which he spread the good news of God's generous forgiveness in his day. Many of his parables make the same point. God is like a shepherd seeking a lost sheep (Luke 15:3–7). God is willing to give hired workers what they need to live, a living wage, even if they have only just joined the work force (Matt 20:1–16). God is like the Samaritan who cares about the injured man on the road (Luke 10:25–37).

In all these parables Jesus is talking both about himself and about God. They are, he claims, on the same page. Explicitly he declares forgiveness of sins to people already during his ministry, such as the woman who anointed him (Luke 7:47–49) and to the paralytic (Mark 2:5), where Mark has him declare: "For the Son of Man has authority on earth to forgive sins" (2:10). The prayer he taught his disciples, the Lord's Prayer, has them pray for forgiveness in the faith of receiving it already there and then.

Jesus told parables about the implications of receiving God's forgiveness (Matt 18:23–35). We need to forgive others if God is to forgive us (Matt 6:14–15; Mark 11:25), even 77 times (Matt 18:21–22). At no point did he intimate that he was talking about a forgiveness that would only be available after he had died on the cross.

Nor was Jesus the only one to offer God's forgiveness. John the Baptist, too, challenged people to turn to God and to let him immerse them in God's cleansing forgiveness, represented in the rivers of the Jordan River (Mark 1:4–5). The Psalms also celebrate the generosity of God's forgiveness (e.g., Psalm 51). Forgiveness was simply part of what it meant to have a relationship with God, and it belonged to the good news that Jesus preached and acted out, sometimes directly offering God's forgiveness. It was always at the heart of Jewish faith, which in the Psalms acclaimed God's love and mercy as enduring forever.

It is simply not true that before Jesus died there was no forgiveness of sins. How then did it come about that very early in the movement we find Christians claiming that Christ died for our sins and, using images of sacrifice and dying for others to declare their faith, then going on to claim that this alone achieved forgiveness of sins? It all has to do with the way they tried to make sense of an overwhelming event.

The Execution of Jesus

The cross, the death of Jesus, was much more than a point marking the end of Jesus' life. It was a horrific, cruel event. How on earth could Jesus come to such a terrible end? How could the first believers come to terms with such an event? To understand what confronted them we need to appreciate the circumstances that brought it about.

Execution by crucifixion was a Roman practice designed to deter offenders, especially enemies of the regime. Seeing birds picking out the eyes of the condemned and dogs jumping up and pulling off the legs and seeing the wretched state of the victim worked effectively to strike terror into would-be revolutionaries. When Pilate crucified Jesus, he did so on the basis that Jesus was a threat to the regime, not by force of arms, otherwise he would have rounded up his followers, but by force of ideas.

Whether from Jesus' own lips or those of others, the claim that Jesus was the Messiah, even a non-violent one, was enough. He was put in the category of subversives to be just another one to be executed for all to see. As he was put into that category, so he was put alongside two other subversives. Older translations that describe them as "thieves" miss the point. The Greek word also means revolutionaries and must mean that also here.

It is consistent with this understanding that we find the story of Barabbas, a rebel, being offered as a swap for Jesus, to mark an alleged practice of releasing one prisoner each year on Passover weekend. It is also why the charge attached to the cross read, "King of the Jews." That was another way of describing the hope of the Messiah who would like David be a king of his people. For Pilate it was mockery and ridicule. Faith would later see it as true—in a very different sense.

Nothing suggests that Jesus was intent on violent revolution, but he did proclaim the hope of good news for the poor and hungry. His teachings about the kingdom or reign of God held before people the prospect of a very different society from the one over which Rome and its agents ruled. Thus, it will have been much more than simply the title, "Messiah," that would have annoyed the Romans. His disrupting the temple might have been the last straw and would have offended not only the temple authorities but also the Romans who were proud to defend it as one of their concessions to their subjects.

The Romans were impatient of the many such movements of the time, which they saw as destabilizing the vulnerable eastern flank of their empire. Administratively the neatest response was to tidy away such trouble with swift violence. Jesus was not the only one treated in this way. Act swiftly and decisively. Stop any such movement before it gets out of hand, like squashing ants.

Dealing with the Shame and Despair

Imagine the shame and despair the disciples would have felt. Crucifixion was an ignominious death designed to shame. That was, as we know, not the end. As we will discuss in greater detail elsewhere, Peter claimed to have seen a vision of Jesus alive and soon the message spread, generating a variety of stories about seeing Jesus appear and disappear and about women finding his tomb empty. But they still had to come to terms with what had happened to Jesus.

Grief is something we all experience. Pain is pain. Sometimes it is simply like receiving a wound. Keep it clean. Give it time. It will heal. There are many ways that grief can go wrong: when we refuse to accept the reality of what has happened, when we won't let ourselves cry, when we blame others or blame ourselves. Sometimes we face pain in tragic events or the loss of significant figures and we wonder. How does one, for instance, process events like the assassination of Gandhi or the execution of Dietrich Bonhoeffer?

For the first believers, steeped in their Jewish faith, Jesus' death was like the death of prophets, killed for their courage to speak the truth. It was also the fate that some writers of the Psalms wrote of, writers who then celebrated vindication. Psalm 22, in particular, became a rich resource for reflection. As the righteous of old suffered rejection and humiliation, so did Jesus.

In early accounts of Jesus' execution this Psalm played a key role in helping them fill out the scant details available to them. Its first verse, "My God, my God, why have you forsaken me?", comes on the lips of Jesus. Perhaps Jesus really did say this. Perhaps those who told the story imagined that this was the kind of thing he would have said. In any case it was not an academic thesis about whether God was present or not, but a very human cry of pain.

Two more motifs come into the retelling from Psalm 22: the mockery and the dividing up of his clothes. "All who see me mock at me; they make mouths at me, they shake their heads; Commit your cause to the Lord; let him deliver—let him rescue the one in whom he delights" (22:7–8). Thus, in Mark's version of the story, our earliest account, we read:

> Those who passed by derided him, shaking their heads and saying, "Aha! You who would destroy the temple and build it in three days, save yourself, and come down from the cross!" In the same way the chief priests, along with the scribes, were also mocking him among themselves and saying, "He saved others; he cannot save himself. Let the Messiah, the King of Israel, come down from the cross now, so that we may see and believe." Those who were crucified with him also taunted him. (15:29–32)

Similarly, the psalmist writes: "They divide my clothes among themselves, and for my clothing they cast lots" (22:18). And so, according to Mark's story, they did:

> And they crucified him, and divided his clothes among them, casting lots to decide what each should take. (15:25)

Did they really? Or was this what those telling the story imagined might have happened on the basis of the psalm? Such free imaginative writing may account for the allusion also to Psalm 69 similarly in the account in the Gospel according to John where we read:

> After this, when Jesus knew that all was now finished, he said (in order to fulfill the scripture), "I am thirsty." A jar full of sour wine was standing there. So they put a sponge full of the wine on a branch of hyssop and held it to his mouth. When Jesus had received the wine, he said, "It is finished." Then he bowed his head and gave up his spirit. (John 19:28–30)

For my thirst they gave me vinegar to drink. (Ps 69:21)

How much actually happened and how much is elaboration based on these psalms is debated. What is, however, clear is that by seeing Jesus' death in the light of what happened to the prophets and what the righteous of the Psalms faced, people could see Jesus' death as standing in continuity with Scripture, in that sense fulfilling it.

"Christ died for our sins" (1 Cor 15:3)

It defied their faith to surrender to a notion that God was not present in the event of Jesus' death or that Rome had outmaneuvered God. God was there. God surely was there. In the process of appropriating what had happened, new possibilities arose. It was the common belief that since Adam people died because of their sin and their death was a sufficient penalty to pay for it.

The death of a very good person would, they believed, achieve more. The death of a righteous person could let loose a surplus of goodness that brought benefit to others. This was the case with the Jewish heroes who were executed by the Syrian king Antiochus Epiphanes in the early second century BCE when the people of Jerusalem rose up against his oppressive regime in the so-called Maccabean revolt. Their martyrdoms were seen as not only on behalf of the people, but also as having unleashed benefit, which also in that sense covered their sins (2 Macc 7).

More well-known is the passage in Isaiah 53, where the prophet depicts the suffering and death of a person who was truly righteous and God's servant. The prophet declares: "He was wounded for our transgressions" (53:5) and even sees this as God's own doing. Whether processing the dilemma of his people's suffering or reflecting a real or imaginary individual, the figure would later inspire interpretations of Jesus' death, but before it did, there were already developments in this direction.

All this led to the conclusion that surely Jesus' death could also be seen as similarly producing benefit. He was like the Maccabean martyrs and the figure in Isaiah 53. Even more so, the community of believers had made the transition from hopeless despair to new life, represented in what they described as the coming of the Spirit. Luke connects this for symbolic reasons to the Feast of Pentecost 50 days after Passover (Acts 2), but elsewhere it is represented as occurring much earlier. The Gospel according to John, for instance, depicts the risen Jesus as giving the disciples the gift of the Spirit on the evening of resurrection day itself (20:22).

Thus, it was possible to conclude that Jesus' death was indeed much more than an end and an execution. It started something new. It unleashed benefit now available to all. So they could now acclaim with confidence: "Christ died for our sins," adding "according to the scriptures." This is how Paul tells us that the gospel summary was passed on to him (1 Cor 15:3–5).

Making such a claim was never meant to deny that God's forgiveness was present already in the ministries of Jesus and John the Baptis—and in their common Jewish faith—any more than acclaiming the deaths of the Maccabean martyrs and the servant of Isaiah 53 required the abandonment of all other means of receiving God's forgiveness. Over time people did tend to lose sight of this.

Christ's Death as a Sacrifice

The world of the New Testament was a world where temples and cults played a significant role. Whether sacrifices in the Jerusalem temple or sacrifices in temples and at pagan shrines, people simply assumed that sacrifices did something. Some saw them as ways of appeasing or paying off an angry deity and buying favor, but mostly no such reflection accompanied the act. Sacrifices simply worked. They had an effect. Thus, it is no surprise that people began to speak of Jesus' death, not only as on behalf of others and bringing them benefit, vicarious in the technical sense, but also as a sacrifice.

We find, indeed, that the early believers came to use a wide range of images to talk about Jesus' death and its impact. It was like a sacrifice, whether one of the daily sacrifices, a sacrifice that inaugurated an agreement or covenant, or one of the Atonement Day sacrifices as elaborated in the letter to the Hebrews. In addition it seems that the Passover lamb, not originally understood as a sacrifice for sins but a celebration of Israel's liberation from Egypt, came to be understood in this way. Originally in the story of Israel's liberation the blood on the doorposts was to ward off the angel of death. The imagination could also take this image to depict Jesus' death as warding off the devil and so liberating people from Satan's grasp, even portraying it as a great victory over death.

These were all images designed to give expression to the faith that Jesus' death was not in vain but was "for us." As images they belong in the realm of poetry, where they all in different ways convey the same central message. They are not statements of prose, let alone definitions of what happened, and so are no more to be read this way than we should read love poetry as making scientific statements. "You are the apple of my eye" is not a statement about fruit.

As the Christian movement grew and society developed, what were once images reflecting the cultic assumptions of the ancient world came to be treated more literally. This created many difficulties, not only in how to synthesize all these diverse images together, but also in what a literal reading of them might do to our understanding of God.

When Israel, for instance used the image of redemption and ransom to claim that God redeemed or ransomed Israel from Egypt (e.g., Ps 72:15), this was imagery. They did not accompany such statements with explanations such as that God paid a ransom to someone, to pharaoh or the devil, in order to buy Israel free. That would have been absurd. And when redemption imagery is used to describe the liberating of Jesus' life and death, the intention was almost certainly not to suggest that God thereby paid a ransom to the devil or that Jesus paid a ransom to God or some other complex explanation. It was simply imagery of liberation.

Similarly, ideas of dying for others could be read quite literally. Did Jesus pay the penalty that God was demanding for everyone's sins, taking their punishment and so persuading God to change course and forgive people, like the elder brother in the fake news version of the prodigal son parable with which this chapter began? That would indeed produce an image of God who was not on the same page as Jesus. That would mean God is not normally loving and forgiving but did a deal with Jesus to make an exception to God's normal ways of operating. This, too, is absurd, though it is alive and well in many forms of Christian piety.

Again, did seeing Jesus' death as a sacrifice carry with it the notion that Jesus averted God's anger? God was offended and outraged at human sin. How could God ever forgive without surrendering sound principles and divine integrity? Jesus persuaded God to change and helped God make the transition by paying off the debt. God's accounting was satisfied. Now God could forgive. The deal was done. This is also preposterous and portrays God as quite the opposite of how Jesus spoke of God. It is all too human in the worst sense.

Reading the Poetry

Often such literal language appears in our traditions, not least in the poetry of our hymns and songs. People will often sing songs and say prayers couched in these terms without analyzing what they might imply if taken literally and the awful picture of God they paint. This calls for tolerance and understanding. For the same person who claims Christ paid the penalty for our sins may have a profound understanding of God who is loving and generous and not see the contradiction that such expressions embody. There is no room for condemnation here. Nevertheless, there is room for self-critical reflection, especially among those who frame and compose our worship. Otherwise the message we embody can unwittingly be opposite to the gospel we intend.

Ultimately, what the first believers declared with their reflections on Jesus' death is not different from what Jesus already declared by word and action in his ministry, namely that God confronts us with the possibility of being loved and forgiven and beginning anew to embrace radical love in the world, even when it may cost us dearly. Christ's life declares it and his death declares it and God through resurrection affirms it, not because Jesus converted God to a different way of thinking, but because love is at the heart of God's being, as love is at the heart of every caring parent.

For Reflection: How can we continue using language about Jesus' death as "for us" and "for sins" without letting it say things about God that we do not believe?

3

Does the Cross Mean "No"?

Love is the way and the truth and the life.
No one comes to the Father except by love.
(with apologies to John 14:6)

IN 1959 THE BILLY Graham Crusade in Auckland, my home town in New Zealand, had me learn texts from Romans that summed up the gospel: "All have sinned" (3:23); "The wages of sin is death but the gift of God is eternal life" (6:23) (death means hell; eternal life means heaven). For by sending Jesus to die for our sins God made forgiveness possible (John 3:16). The message is clear for all: repent or you will go to hell. I can remember in the enthusiasm of my teenage years when I began to preach that I sensed some parts of the New Testament did not put the message in this way. It could be made to fit John's Gospel quite well, the favorite Gospel in such circles, but not so well the other Gospels. I can remember thinking they were not "evangelical" enough because they did not appear to make this message central. I think what I sensed about them was, indeed, correct, but I was confident. I knew what to preach.

The message that salvation and forgiveness came to humanity only through the death of Christ, as noted in the previous chapter, had widespread implications and these were exclusive. At its simplest it implied that before this event the world was in waiting. The cross implies "No!" There was no forgiveness or salvation for the people of Israel before Jesus died nor for anyone else. Elaborated, it meant ever since Adam human beings have sinned and so deserve death, indeed, condemnation to the eternal fires of hell. When Jesus offered himself as a sacrifice for the sins of the world, he opened for people the possibility of reconciliation with God, who would no longer plan to send them to hell, but would welcome them to heaven.

Therefore, the cross meant yes, to the possibility of forgiveness and no, to all other claims about forgiveness. According to the letter to the Hebrews, even the faithful of Israel were left waiting to enter heaven until Jesus' death opened the gate (11:39–40). John's Gospel has Jesus declare unambiguously: "I am the way and the truth and the life. No one comes to the Father except through me" (14:6). And Luke has Peter declare in the book of Acts: "There is salvation in no one else, for there is no other name under heaven given among mortals by which we must be saved" (4:12).

The logic of Paul's account of the gospel, which he preaches and which he is commending to the believers in Rome as acceptable and authoritative, appears to be the same. Accordingly, God has brought all of humanity, both Jews and gentiles into condemnation because of their sin, and only through the intervention of God's goodness could this be reversed (Rom 3:19–26). Paul's view may not be quite so exclusive, because he can contemplate that Abraham was also right with God because of his faith (Rom 4:1–5).

Forgiveness Monopoly

The evidence suggests that there was a widespread view in early Christianity that they alone could offer salvation, understood as forgiveness of sins, and this was because of Christ's death on the cross. This became especially important as the focus moved away from what were Jesus' primary concerns, which presupposed forgiveness of sins as an element of caring like healing, to a message about surviving the judgment to come and not being sent to hell. For this reconfigured gospel, forgiveness of sins, rather than being presupposed as an element of the message, became the message itself. If we look at that shift, we can see that it presents serious problems.

Jesus, himself, framed his good news as the promise of the coming reign of God (Mark 1:15), which would be good news for the poor and hungry (Luke 6:20–21). It was about a transformed society where God was at the center challenging people to embrace love. He challenged people to repent, thus changing direction, abandoning sin and receiving forgiveness, and to believe the good news, namely, to embrace this vision for themselves and for others. As we have seen forgiveness of sins was not an innovation in his message, but a key element of Jewish faith that his message presupposed.

Having repented, people were then to embrace the good news. Forgiveness of sins, like healing, was part of what the good news entailed but good news for the poor and for all was also much wider than that. Jesus' favorite image for what this good news meant was that of a great feast where there would be room for all who responded to the invitation to belong (Luke 14:16–24). His special meals of belonging with his disciples came to symbolize that vision and was remembered and re-enacted in what we now celebrate in stylized form as Holy Communion, the Eucharist (Mark 14:22–25).

The shift from his Jewish world in Galilee and Judea to the wider world of the Roman empire coincided with a shift in the way of presenting the gospel. It became less focused on communal renewal, transformation, and the vision of God's kingdom as belonging and more focused on the fate of individuals at the final judgment. In some ways this made sense because Jesus' message was so much connected to the communal hopes for liberation of Jewish people in Galilee and Judea. People in Corinth, for instance, would have little interest in promises to people in Palestine.

Similarly, a term like Messiah, even when reconfigured along the lines of Jesus' vision for change, was too Jewish and would make little sense in the non-Jewish world. The focus on escaping condemnation on the day of judgment was of greater universal appeal. It was also simpler. Love was still there in its message when understood in this way: "For God so loved the world that he gave his only Son, that everyone who believes in him may not perish but may have eternal life" (John 3:16). It became a message about not perishing (i.e., going to hell) and gaining eternal life (i.e., going to heaven). Even to put it this way partly distorts John 3:16, because "eternal life" in John does not mean heaven, but life already in the here and now with God that continues beyond death.

This new neat exclusive message of individual salvation based on Christ's achievement on the cross, forgiveness of sins, and escape from hell was not without its problems. One was that it largely lost the communal dimension so central to Jesus' message. The hope of the kingdom of God was a communal hope, not a hope focused primarily on the individual. The other major problem was the fact that the evidence we have, as noted in the previous chapter, makes it unambiguously clear that Jesus already offered forgiveness of sins during his ministry, in his parables, his sayings and his actions. Mark makes it very clear: "The Son of Man has authority on earth to forgive sins" (2:10). The Lord's Prayer, which is very Jewish, assumes that

God hears people when they pray for forgiveness. This was a standard element of Jewish faith. To treat it as something new and therefore as the main element in Jesus' message of good news produced a distortion.

Mark would, I am sure, be surprised, if we were to say to him that the gospel was primarily about forgiveness of sins. I am sure he would point to John the Baptist and say, "But have you not read the opening section of my Gospel?" John was already offering universal forgiveness of sins. Jesus never denied that John the Baptist offered forgiveness, indeed to all who would allow themselves to be immersed in God's goodness (Mark 1:4–5). The new thing about Jesus according to Mark was that he would baptize people with the Spirit (1:8). Mark might go on to explain that Jesus did this by bringing the Spirit of God into people's lives with healing, forgiveness, and renewal. He might even repeat the warning he has Jesus bring in 3:28–29, when in referring to his ministry Jesus declares that not to recognize the Spirit in his ministry is indeed unforgiveable blasphemy.

The exclusive claims we noted above that limit forgiveness to something available only after Jesus' death are in danger therefore of also excluding Jesus' own offering of forgiveness during his ministry and denying what the Scripture says about John the Baptist and the faith of Israel. How could it come to this, that even Jesus' own ministry is disqualified? There is something seriously wrong about such thinking. There was something seriously wrong about my thinking. How could it go so wrong?

The answer lies in part on the shift of focus, noted above, as believers moved out of the Jewish context of Jesus' message. They would not have understood themselves as wanting to exclude Jesus. Their primary reason for the exclusive claims is that they wanted to claim that they had something unique not available anywhere else. They had a monopoly on forgiveness and so salvation, but that was in danger of leaving out central elements in Jesus' message. The desire to claim to have the sole source of forgiveness and so salvation was in that sense market driven. They felt they had to disqualify all other alternatives.

Competition and Conflict

We know that there were at the time also followers of John the Baptist. In some circles, such as those where the Gospel according to John was written, this meant that Christ believers felt a need to disqualify John the Baptist and his circle. Accordingly, John's Gospel no longer depicts John the Baptist as offering forgiveness of sins and as fulfilling the role of Elijah as in the other Gospels. Instead it reduces him to being simply a witness pointing to Jesus. It shows John the Baptist almost falling over backwards to deny such claims.

> This is the testimony given by John when the Jews sent priests and Levites from Jerusalem to ask him, "Who are you?" 20He confessed and did not deny it, but confessed, "I am not the Messiah." 21And they asked him, "What then? Are you Elijah?" He said, "I am not." "Are you the prophet?" He answered, "No." (1:19–20)

The triple assertion, "confessed and did not deny it, but confessed," makes it plain that a lot was at stake.

The main rivals for the first believers were, however, their fellow Jews who refused to join them. At some point the Jews of the Jesus movement decided to deny that Jewish faith provided a means of finding forgiveness and having a right relationship with God. Because of what they claimed about the cross, they said No. No salvation or forgiveness in Judaism.

As one can imagine, the denial that there was salvation and forgiveness in Judaism would have led to bitter disputes. The commitment to exclusiveness held. Judaism, the faith of Jesus, and the faith that gave birth to the movement was from now on, in effect, disqualified. The determination to disqualify Judaism or other Jews was so strong that it does not appear to have occurred to them that the effect was to disqualify not only their fellow Jews but, therefore, also Jesus, himself, and his ministry.

The bitterness of these disputes reflects the fact that this was for many a dispute as close to home as could be. Sadly, it led to shaming and blaming and hurt typical of conflicts with one's own. We return to this in more detail in chapter 8 below. The anger and resentment that these fellow Jews refused the message of the Jesus movement led to serious recriminations. In telling the stories of Jesus' conflicts with his fellow Jews, these believing Jews and the non-Jews who rapidly joined the expanding movement increasingly engaged in stereotypes. As a result many of the stories of conflict between Jesus and some of his contemporaries over application of God's law now come to us as irreconcilable and harsh contrasts reflecting their use in these conflicts of later times.

There is even a trend towards shifting the blame onto the Jews for the death of Jesus and depicting Pilate as innocent or at least weak in giving way to their demands. In Matthew's Gospel, which carries much bitterness and anger belonging to these disputes, this trend reaches its saddest point where Matthew has the Jerusalem crowd declare: "His blood be upon us and our children" (27:53). People listening to Matthew's Gospel would have known of the horrors of the capture of Jerusalem by the Romans in 70 CE, perhaps a decade and a half before Matthew wrote, when many lost their lives. Matthew, indeed, depicts this as God's judgment on the city's people for rejecting Jesus and those sent to them (22:1–14).

Another painful development meets us in John's Gospel with its freely composed speeches and dialogues designed to reflect key issues of the author's time but now pictured as happening in larger than life scenes during Jesus' earthly ministry. John 8 has Jesus declare Jews who refused his gospel as children of the devil (8:44). The intent appears to be to declare all Jews not submitting to the gospel as evil captives of Satan. Love has turned to hatred and the consequences in history have been horrendous. We return to these fateful developments in chapter 8.

In the world of competing claims where the new movement sought to profile itself and claim uniqueness, such excesses were understandable. They should, however, be recognized as serious departures from what was at the heart of Jesus' gospel. The exposition of the cross as unleashing life need not have been treated as a basis for excluding others, let alone for excluding Jesus himself. There was no need to say, No, to Judaism and certainly no need, in effect, to say, No, to Jesus.

Love and Light

Did the cross mean no? Yes, it did in the hands of many. Did the cross need to mean no? Not if we understand how all this developed. The cross needs to be seen not as an event separate from the ministry of Jesus, but as bringing to expression, indeed to a climax, what his ministry entailed. That was about radical love and a radical vision of change. The cross brought a conflict to a head. The call to love and change met the callous response of a totalitarian regime. Embodying sin, it executed such love and hope—as such regimes regularly do.

In doing so, Rome's response symbolizes the rejection of love, indeed of God. It becomes a revelation of evil. At the same time the cross becomes a revelation of love, the love that Jesus embodied and advocated to the end. In that sense the cross reveals simultaneously love and hate. The impact of its symbolism of love is profound and found expression in a rich and diverse range of images, whose poetry spoke to their age and many still speak and inspire.

This event outside Jerusalem's walls in first-century Judea still resounds in worlds far and wide, wherever people see love and see hate. One of love's richest images is that it is like light. The light shines to bring growth, to show the way, to bring safety and security, but it also shines to expose, to reveal, to confront. People across the world recognize love because it is an essential aspect of our humanity. This is why Jesus appeals to parenting when he defends it.

Wherever love is, there is life and hope. Love as light wears no labels and we learn to recognize it wherever it occurs. There is never any need to say "no" to love's light. That includes whether it occurs in your own religion and culture or that of others.

Paradoxically John's Gospel, which contains hate speech, also contains love speech and employs universal images to celebrate it: not only light, but bread and water and life. These are images known across many cultures and religions. And interestingly, John's Gospel uses such images not in a restrictive way as though they came into existence only after Jesus' death, but as belonging to his being as the Word, as God's self-expression. Indeed, that Gospel's depiction of Jesus makes him so much a bearer of God's being that effectively everything special it says of Jesus is equally what is said of God.

In effect, what the author of John's Gospel claims of Jesus he is really claiming about God. Christians then claimed that Jesus was and is indeed an aspect of God, not a second god, nor god instead of God, but like a window on God. "In the beginning was the Word, and the Word was with God, and the Word was God" (1:1). God is that Gospel's central theme and everything said of Jesus is subordinated to that theme. The effect is to present us with an understanding of God as light and life, bread and water, or as a slightly later writer from the same context, the author of 1 John, declared, "God is love" (4:7).

We can recognize the light of love wherever it shines. Luke paints a picture of Paul in Athens that reflects a surprising openness. In it he has Paul acknowledge that his Athenian listeners also know God. Indeed, he cites the poet Aratus to this effect—"We are all God's children—and adds those profound words about God as the one "in whom we live and move and have our being" (Acts 17:28). That did not mean that he decided not to speak about Jesus. On the contrary, it was why he then went on to speak of him. Openness to awareness of God in other cultures is no reason to remain silent about the revelation of love in Christ, but it does recognize some common ground.

Approached in this way there is no need for defensive exclusivity. We can hold hands with and celebrate love wherever it occurs. In that sense the cross does not say, No. It says, Yes, and invites us to communion with all from whatever culture or religion who celebrate it. That may sound overly generous and permissive, but, on the contrary, it is sharply critical and potentially dangerous, as Jesus experienced. For the light of love exposes hatred and injustice wherever it occurs, in whatever religion or culture, and calls us to rise about sectional loyalties to its embrace.

We can then say, "Love is the way and the truth and the life. No one comes to the Father except by love" (with apologies to John 14:6). And, indeed, for that reason we affirm that God was in Christ, because that is where we have learned this to be so.

For Reflection: How can we both affirm the significance of Christ's death and affirm inclusivity? What are the implications for relating to religions other than our own and including Judaism?

SECTION B

Hope: What Can Love Hope For?

4

Will God Stop Loving?

Give thanks to the Lord for God is good.
God's love endures until the day of judgment and then stops
(with apologies to the psalmists)

THE IDEA THAT LOVE will last forever is fragile. It is alas human to want to impose limits. What if my love is rejected? "I hate you! Why don't you love me!" is not an uncommon cry—and it comes out of love, hurt love. Vengeance is something bigger. Anger has its roots in pain and hurt and easily becomes hate and retaliation. The Sermon on the Mount challenges such hate in its deeper exposition of the command not to kill (Matt 5:21–28), but also in its insistence on turning away from retaliation and hatred of enemies (5:38–48).

When it declares that we should be "perfect" as God is "perfect" (5:48), this perfection is primarily not about quantity but about quality, not flawlessness, but a total commitment to love. Luke's shorter version uses not the word "perfect," but the word "merciful" or "compassionate": "Be compassionate, as your heavenly Father is compassionate" (6:36). These words attributed to Jesus were not a new invention. They are at the heart of Israel's faith. Matthew depicts them as part of Jesus' upholding of biblical law.

Love and Justice

Does love and compassion mean there should be no justice system, no courts, no police force? Is love about tolerating anything and everything?

Clearly, not. It is love that requires we have laws that protect people, for instance, from violence, and that sometimes means we need to forcibly prevent such violence, indeed even restrain such perpetrators often to the extent of removing them from the community for a time. We need courts. We need rules. We need penalties that deter those who endanger themselves and others by speeding, for instance.

Do we need hate? Is the justice system a legal means whereby a community can hate wrongdoers? Hardly, but sometimes we can hear it that way when media sources report crimes, and those who suffer from crimes of violence and abuse cry out for vengeance. One could even say that the justice system is designed to make sure that the hate does not go too far.

Such approaches to justice in the community stand in stark contradiction to approaches that see the justice system as a necessary instrument to bring protection and to care for people. At its best the justice system not only confronts wrongdoing and where necessary restrains wrongdoers, even in custody, but seeks to rehabilitate such wrongdoers and bring them back to healthy behavior. In this there are stories of success and stories of failure.

The core of this healthy approach to justice is that it does not act out of hate but out of caring for and respecting the person. This is the reason why legislatures based on such principles have rejected capital punishment, because that effectively gives up on people and embraces a response to crime based on hate or at least on punishment with no prospect or intent of bringing change. It is a giving up of love and respect, as is the angry cry that authorities lock some people up and throw away the key.

Justice and Hope

It is surely valid to hope that those who commit violence whether physical or in any other way are brought to account. They should not be allowed to get away with it. This very natural concern is widespread and informs the culture of most communities. It was certainly foundational in the communities of ancient Israel.

The Old Testament as a collection of writings from Israel's past reflects their grappling with what to do about such wrongdoing and also with why sometimes things did go wrong and people suffered. Fortunately, the diverse answers in these diverse writings have come down to us with little if any attempt to harmonize the differences, indeed, the contradictions. Some writers held the view that bad things happen to bad people and good things happen to good people and that God is in charge of this. Some of the histories even depict the nation as falling to defeat by surrounding nations when it turned away from God and winning victories when they repented and turned back to God. The righteous prosper; the wicked do not.

There were others who took a more realistic view and acknowledged that sometimes the wicked prospered and the righteous suffered. The book of Job reflects some grappling with these issues and indeed includes different and conflicting explanations of why Job suffered. Its editorial frame favors the view that Job's suffering was not because he was bad, but then interprets it as imposed as a test by God.

Similarly, the suffering of the one called God's servant in Isaiah 53 is depicted not as happening because he was bad, but as brought about by God. Such a view rests on the notion that God controls all events and causes them to occur. This, too, ran into difficulties. God surely does not cause violence and abuse. The nations that some alleged were God's instruments for punishing Israel for its sin were, as some like Ezekiel came to recognize, also very sinful, indeed much more so.

The reality was that some people and some nations and groups did get away with violence and injustice and there was little prospect that they would ever be held to account. That may seem pessimistic, but it made sense. The more the thinkers in the Jewish faith were exposed to the machinations of the wider world, especially through being incorporated in the successive empires of the Persians, the Greeks, and the Romans, the more such conclusions were inevitable.

God was not controlling all the events, but did this mean there was never any prospect of people and nations being held to account for their actions? The answer that emerged from their thinking and became dominant was that there would be a day of reckoning at some time in the future, and in the eyes of many, in the very near future. This could only be possible if God directly intervened to sort out the mess.

Thus, people began to look to a day of judgment when God would call all to account, the living but also the dead. For this to happen the dead would need to be brought back to life. The traditional understanding had been that when people died, their spirits entered the abode of the shades, called Sheol or Hades, and were all but nonexistent, sometimes referred to as like chirping birds, not really alive at all, but also not totally dead (Job 7:7–10; Ps 6:5; Isa 8:19; 38:18).

Two beliefs led to new thoughts about the dead and both were about fairness. Surely the righteous who had suffered deserved some reward. Thus, we begin to see the belief that at some point in the future they would be raised from the dead. To be alive again they needed a body, but it needed to be a superior body that was not vulnerable to the problems of their earthly body. Thus, we find dreams of the righteous being raised from the dead in shining bodies like the stars (Dan 12:3). Some dreamt of all the righteous, those still alive and those raised from the dead, forming one happy community.

The other belief arose from the fact that to hold people to account, and especially the wicked who had since died, they would also need to have bodies. You cannot speak or see or hear without a body. Thus, there developed the notion that all would be raised from the dead and all would have to stand before God and be judged on the basis of what they had done in their lives (Dan 12:2). By the time of Jesus such beliefs were widely held. They are therefore also part of the world of Jesus and his contemporaries and of the Jesus movement. Jesus' vision of the reign of God reflects this framework of thought, which he then adapted to claim that this ideal community of belonging and caring could already come into reality when people opened themselves to God in this world.

Fantasies of Terror

Belief that there must be accountability is one thing. Imagining how this might be is another. One popular notion was that the wicked to be judged by God would suffer punishment. They envisaged this not as corrective punishment or with a view to rehabilitation, but as permanent punishment. Indeed, some pictured God's justice as sending people into a situation where they would be permanently subjected to excruciating pain, often as being kept alive to experience being burned, indeed forever (Matt 13:41–43; 25:46; Rev 19:20). This is a far cry from the notion of justice discussed earlier, based on respect and caring.

Inevitably some will have developed their fantasies of terror as a result of their own pain and their desire for vengeance.

> I saw under the altar the souls of those who had been slaughtered for the word of God and for the testimony they had given; 10they cried out with a loud voice, 'Sovereign Lord, holy and true, how

long will it be before you judge and avenge our blood on the inhabitants of the earth?' (Rev 6:9–10)

Some have defended such violence on the basis that while it is inappropriate for any human to inflict it, because all humans are also sinners, it is right for God to do so, because God is good. God set the standards, the laws, and God set the punishments. God warned that people committing sin would be punished, so now they are to be punished. This is justice. God is consistent and good.

Such fantasies of terror have inspired images of hell. And while for some it has been with glee that they contemplate their enemies exposed to such terrible torture, for others the prospect has caused great pain and inspired their compassion to preach to sinners and tell them that they can be saved from hell if only they believe in Jesus. In effect, the message implies that we can be saved from God, or to put it in more complex terms: God in love has sent Jesus to save us from the torments God plans to inflict on sinners. That makes little sense.

It did, however, make sense to me as a teenage evangelist. It was what I was to preach, warning people of the wrath to come. It bothered me that my minister of whom I was fond, seemed not to preach like this. Surely it was straightforward. People are in danger. Tell them there is a way of escape. I used to dismiss his views as watering down the gospel.

The underlying assumption in such constructions is that God will indeed stop loving and that God is quite happy to engage in such violence, exposing unbelievers to an eternal experience of terrible pain. There are New Testament texts that can be cited to support such an idea and there are many Christians who still believe this about God.

Such an idea jars, however, with notions of justice that human societies now recognize as appropriate. Endless violence against a person is an appalling infringement of human rights and the opposite of love. The belief that it is acceptable for God to behave like this because God is righteous has inspired many, mostly men, to claim the same right in engaging in domestic and other violence when they claim to be right and righteous.

More importantly, such violent notions jar with an understanding of God as loving and with the teachings in the Sermon on the Mount about loving both neighbors and enemies. Of course, this contradiction is present in the Sermon on the Mount itself, which, as elsewhere in Matthew, threatens hellfire to the dissenters and disobedient (5:21–28). Christian

WHAT CAN LOVE HOPE FOR?

faith purveys both stances and both stances have impacted on human history for worse and for better.

Do we hope for accountability? Yes, we can, but it must never be at the expense of compassion and must be based on a notion of justice that we have long since learned, partly on the basis of the gospel itself and partly on the basis of the wisdom of thinking and caring people, is abhorrent. In this we have made God in our own image and so enshrined what must be acknowledged as evil.

> "Give thanks to the Lord for God is good. God's love endures until the day of judgment and then stops". (with apologies to the psalmists)

No. Rather let the original texts stand:

> Give thanks to the Lord for God is good. God's love endures forever! (Ps 100:5; 106:1; 107:1; 118:1–4, 29; 136 as a refrain; 138:8)

Reflection: If the motive for inviting people to become disciples of Christ is not fear of judgment, what is it?

5

What Can Love Hope for?

> Truly I tell you, there are some standing here who will be waiting
> at least 2,000 years before they see the kingdom of God come with
> power. (with apologies to Mark 9:1)

THERE IS A 2,000-YEAR gap between believers in today's twenty-first-century world and those of the first century. For most, there is in addition a major difference in culture, information, and, of course, language. To engage the writings of the New Testament is to engage in a cross-cultural encounter with all the respect and opportunity for learning and enrichment which that entails.

I can remember as a child that when I heard people speak of "Bible Times," I thought of something that belonged to another world, to a golden age. The heroes of the Bible might as well have lived on a different planet. They were at least far away in time and space. Then I needed to go through the kind of realization that the world of scholarship on the Bible went through a few centuries ago. For them it was the growing realization that the world of ancient Greece and Rome they studied in the classics was the same world in which the first Christians lived.

From figures of fantasy and abstraction the Bible's heroes became for me, as it did for them, real people in space and time, who needed to be approached with the same historical sensitivity we bring to research on Alexander the Great or Julius Caesar. They lived in our world, our history, and in the scheme of things, as we now know, not so long ago. We can imagine ourselves back into their world and their thoughts.

In such engagement we are, therefore, meeting people who, if sufficiently informed about the genealogies of the Old Testament, would have told us that the universe came into being 4,000 years before their time in a week of busy creation. Genesis 1–2 was their source of information. They might explain to us how they see this universe, either by telling us about its three-tiered structure of the heavens above and hell beneath and in between the earth as flat or, informed by Greek traditions, might indeed understand the world as a sphere with the sun going around it. There is no need for us to look down our noses at their understandings nor, however, to feel we must embrace them.

We might smile similarly at what was the most common explanation of human reproduction that lay behind the construction of their genealogies, namely that the man sowed the seed (like the egg) into the woman as into a field, by which she nurtured the seed till ready to give birth. Therefore they traced genealogies through males and the tradition of retaining male surnames in part reflects this ancient view. One can hardly blame them for not comprehending the complexities of the process.

Their Hope and Ours?

More significant is the common ground we share with them. That, for believers, includes making Jesus and his message central to our understanding of God and what it means to live in relationship to God. It also includes believing in love and hope. But there, with hope, the difficulties begin, and we need to sort out what still inspires and makes sense from what we must respectfully treat as a view they held that is for many reasons no longer viable today.

To begin with the most obvious, when they expected the kingdom of God (Mark 9:1) and the return of Jesus in their lifetime, as did Paul, for instance (1 Cor 15:51–52; 1 Thess 4:15–17), then we have to say, what they imagined did not take place, neither in their lifetime nor in the two millennia that followed. The real Mark 9:1, unlike the one above, read:

> Truly I tell you, there are some standing here who will not taste
> death until they see that the kingdom of God has come with power.

Some try to explain it away as referring to events in Jesus' ministry or the early church, but it is more likely to reflect the widespread view attested in Paul and elsewhere that the last days were upon them. Is it possible to share hope with them, but imagine hope very differently? Surely it is.

The insistent belief that people must be brought to account for their actions, if not in this life, then at some point in the future, as discussed in the previous chapter, shaped how they saw hope. But their hope was for much more than correction and justice in that sense. It was also for justice in a broader sense, namely the establishment of human community where all people are treated with dignity and live in a joyous open relationship with God.

In a world where access to abundant food was far from the norm, people looked forward to special occasions where families and friends would gather for special meals. In some sense, what for most in the developed parts of our world is a daily possibility was for them an exception. It was a special occasion, whether as part of wedding celebrations or as a shared feast in Jerusalem in association with having brought a sacrifice and being able to feast on some of the meat that act made available after the priests took the best portions.

It is, therefore, not surprising that when they imagined hope in the future, they often spoke of it as gathering for such a feast. We see this already in Isaiah's vision of a feast for all peoples:

> On this mountain the Lord of hosts will make for all peoples, a feast of rich food, a feast of well-matured wines, of rich food filled with marrow, of well-matured wines strained clear. (25:6)

That was a very generous vision because it encompassed not just the people of Israel. More common was the limited focus on God's promise for those seen as God's people, Israel. Sometimes they picture the others as coming with the weapons of war and beating swords into ploughs and the spears into pruning hooks (Isa 2:2–4), but mostly the hope was confined to Israel. In some Jewish movements it was defined on the basis of including only those who were part of their group or who were faithful to their interpretation of God's law.

The Hopes of Jesus

It is also not surprising "feast" was the image that Jesus used most to depict future hope, both in parables and in sayings.

37

> Many will come from east and west and will sit at table with Abraham, Isaac, and Jacob in the kingdom of heaven. (Matt 8:11)

Such imagery inspired the parable of the invitation to the great feast (Luke 14:16–24; Matt 22:1–14). When Jesus shared bread and wine with his disciples in his last meal with them, he was not just providing the normal fare for a meal, but foreshadowing the great feast to come, which others, too, saw as a time for drinking good wine and sharing bread, but also much else. Mark reports him as saying:

> Truly I tell you, I will never again drink of the fruit of the vine until that day when I drink it new in the kingdom of God. (14:26)

Jesus gave the opening action of breaking the bread, which a father would perform to give thanks at the beginning of a meal, a very personal meaning, identifying the bread with himself and his impending fate. He did similarly at the end of the meal with the cup of wine (Mark 14:22–24; 1 Cor 11:23–25). The image of the feast served the main message of Jesus—the coming kingdom of God—well.

> The kingdom of God is at hand. Repent and believe the gospel. (Mark 1:15)

We can see something of what this means in the so-called beatitudes where Jesus promises:

> Blessed are you who are poor, for yours is the kingdom of God.
> Blessed are you who are hungry now, for you will be filled.
> Blessed are you who weep now, for you will laugh. (Luke 6:20–21)

When Matthew's revised version speaks of the "poor in spirit" and those hungering for justice (5:3–6), the focus is the same. The dispirited and those longing for justice, including those sharing that longing with them, would find fulfillment of their hope.

Jesus promised "good news for the poor" (Luke 4:16–20; 7:22). That promise was not just about people who had little. It included also sick people and people with disability or mental illness, understood then as demon possession, because anyone like that normally faced a life of poverty.

Jesus' message of good news was not however confined to the needy in terms of economic poverty, but also addressed the rich, like Zacchaeus, the tax collector, and people like him who were noted for already being able to afford rich feasts (Luke 19:1–10). It also addressed others who had similarly marginalized themselves or been marginalized by the more devout in their society, but also those who were marginalized in a broader sense of frequently experiencing discrimination. They could include women, slaves, children, people of other races, beside those who because of their lifestyle were deemed wicked and probably were.

On the basis of the many anecdotes about Jesus incorporated into the gospels and the traditions about his teaching, we can be confident that Jesus proclaimed hope for change and engaged in the process of change during his ministry. He could even claim:

> If I by the Spirit of God cast out demons, then the kingdom of God has come upon you. (Matt 12:28; similarly, Luke 11:20)

Jesus practiced exorcism and other forms of healing, strange to our ears, and gained a reputation for doing such things. Of course, as we shall see in chapter 9 below, such stories often took off and had a life of their own, so that we have to try to see through fantasy and exaggeration. However, even if now obscured, there is a foundation of truth in the claim that he engaged in healing practices and saw these as evidence of what he proclaimed would one day be reality for all.

The same applied to his initiatives to reach out to those in his society who were outcasts or had made themselves outcasts and to give out the message by his words and his actions, that God had not given up on them, even when they might have given up on themselves (Mark 2:15–18; Luke 15:1). There is love and forgiveness in the heart of God. Such undertakings help us understand how Jesus envisaged hope. Thus, when he spoke of the future as a great feast, he envisaged something that would not only feed people and bring them together in harmony and celebration, but would also be inclusive, thus not confined to an elite or the especially devout.

Jesus' vision was for something much larger and encompassing than what he was able to achieve during his ministry where he would have brought change for only a small proportion of the population. More than such micro-change, he proclaimed the good news of macro-change.

Raising such hopes placed Jesus in the category of the enemies of Rome, at least as Rome's agents saw it, Pilate being the local representative. Not an enemy by military means but an enemy by ideas that raised people's hopes for change. As we saw in chapter 2 above, the broad category of subversives was enough to place Jesus alongside two who were probably revolutionaries by force of arms and to have him offered as a swap for another, Barabbas.

Hope and Expectation

The hopes that Jesus lived into reality in a small way during his ministry were real and the expectation of his followers was that they would soon come true in a big way. That was certainly the expectation of John the Baptist whose offer to immerse people in the waters of God's forgiveness was in part on the basis that, as he put it, the axe was already at the base of the tree, the judgment was at hand (3:7–12; Luke 3:7–9).

Matthew even summarizes his message and that of Jesus with the same words: "Repent. The kingdom of heaven is at hand" (3:2; 4:17). It is reasonable to assume that Jesus, too, shared the expectation of John and the disciples after Easter, as indeed of many of the time, that history was reaching a climax and that God would soon intervene. God would reign. Piety tries to make Jesus an exception, but this runs contrary to the evidence. People of hope cited Isaiah's words:

> How beautiful on the mountains are the feet of the messenger who proclaims peace, who brings good tidings, who announces salvation, who declares to Zion, "Your God reigns". (52:7)

When Jesus spoke of the kingdom of God, which meant the reign of God, as being "at hand, near," this was not a claim that it had come and was present wherever he was, with nothing more to be added. Nor was it something that might happen but only within the individual soul. Rather he was claiming that it was soon to break into the world and indeed was already showing signs of its presence when through his actions people were being liberated from the forces that oppressed them.

Jesus spoke the language of his time and shared the presuppositions of his time about the future. This included belief in the day of judgment and in resurrection from the dead of both the good and the bad, and, most notably, the vision of the great feast to which all were invited. That is what lies behind the statement we cited above from Mark 9:1:

> Truly I tell you, there are some standing here who will not taste death until they see that the kingdom of God has come with power.

This is a prediction not of the micro-change evident in the church and the initial successes in the book of Acts, but something much more: macro-change, the inbreaking of God's reign.

Hope and Easter

In the Book of Acts Luke reports that when the disciples came to believe that God had raised Jesus from the dead, they gathered in Jerusalem. This was because Jerusalem was where people expected God would begin the divine reign. They also connected this with the hope that Jesus, himself, would return to be God's agent establishing that reign, God's Messiah. Luke even has Jesus say to the people of Jerusalem that they would face great suffering but then should lift up their heads and see him coming (Luke 21:28) and has Peter on the Day of Pentecost declare of Jesus' resurrection:

> Let the whole house of Israel know with certainty that God has made him Lord and Messiah, this Jesus whom you crucified (Acts 2:36)

In another address he declares:

> Repent therefore, and turn to God so that your sins may be wiped out, 20so that times of refreshing may come from the presence of the Lord, and that he may send the Messiah appointed for you, that is, Jesus, 21who must remain in heaven until the time of universal restoration that God announced long ago through his holy prophets (Acts 3:19–21)

The events we can reconstruct on the basis of the book of Acts and elsewhere enable us to understand how they read Jesus' resurrection. Resurrection was expected as an event at the climax of history. With Jesus' resurrection that climax had begun, so they believed. He was the first to be raised, sometimes even described as the firstborn from the dead (Col 1:18). Similarly, at the climax of history God's Spirit would be poured out in a new way. Accordingly, they interpreted their experience of the Spirit, which Luke portrays as happening on the Feast of Pentecost, as reinforcing their confidence that the end was at hand.

This expectation lived on, at least for the first few generations. Paul writes of the end using traditional imagery belonging to such expectation:

> Listen, I will tell you a mystery! We will not all die, but we will all be changed, 52in a moment, in the twinkling of an eye, at the last

trumpet. For the trumpet will sound, and the dead will be raised imperishable, and we will be changed. (1 Cor 15:51–52)

As noted above, here, as in 1 Thessalonians, he reflects the belief that he would still be alive when this all happens. He has to defend his belief in a resurrection from the dead against people in Corinth who doubted that there was any need for a new embodiment and who probably argued that that the disembodied soul was sufficient. Paul explains that the resurrection body would not be a resuscitated corpse in a physical sense, but spiritual (1 Cor 15:35–49). The physical bodies of those alive would be transfigured, "changed," to become spiritual bodies and the same would happen with the dead at their resurrection.

We see this assumed in descriptions of Jesus' resurrection. His resurrection body has the same spiritual character, enabling him to materialize and dematerialize, passing through closed doors, appearing and then disappearing (Luke 24:31; John 20:19, 26). The belief was not that physical bodies remain corpses and are replaced, but that they are transformed to become this different kind of body without remainder. Hence the conclusion that Jesus' tomb must therefore have been empty.

Luke uses creative artistry to portray the church's beginnings as echoing Israel's history. The pattern he created came to shape the church's calendar right up to the present day. Accordingly, the risen Jesus appears for forty days and then ascends up to where God is (Acts 1:3) and ten days later, at the Feast of Pentecost, of harvest thanksgiving, the Spirit is poured out (Acts 2:1–4).

Luke's artistry is evident there, too, because he models his depiction of the Day of Pentecost on the Jewish legend that when the law was given by God to Moses on Mt. Sinai a flame came down from heaven broke into seventy-two parts, one part for every nation on earth. Only one nation, however, namely Israel, welcomed God's law. Luke's picture plays on this legend but also echoes the legend of the Tower of Babel, told to explain how languages came into being when people arrogantly built a tower to make a name for themselves leading to breakdown in communication symbolized by people speaking different languages. Pentecost reverses that.

Following a literal understanding of Luke's time scheme, people commonly imagine that Jesus' corpse was resuscitated and lived around Jerusalem for forty days and was then removed from earth by ascending up into the heavens. This is not even Luke's view, who depicts Jesus as appearing and disappearing. Luke even preserves evidence that shows his scheme to be something that he imposed on the material because he knows and reports that Jesus also appeared to Paul on the road to Damascus much later. Other writers, however, locate the coming of the Spirit not at the feast of Pentecost, fifty days after Easter, but even as occurring on the very same day as the resurrection, as in John's account, who has Jesus breathe on the disciples, giving them the Spirit, and commission them that evening (20:22).

Imagining Hope

It was inevitable that we have some diversity in the accounts of Christian beginnings. Imagination played a role as well as the artistry of employing symbolism. It is in any case clear that they believed in resurrection and that like Jesus and John the Baptist before them they believed that history was close to its climax. They, therefore, interpreted Jesus' resurrection and their new experience of the Spirit as indicators that they were living in the last days.

When we read these accounts, we not only face the challenges of identifying what were the common elements in the way they interpreted these experiences, what might have been history and what might have been symbolic elaboration. We also have to face the much more serious question of coming to terms with the fact that their expectations failed to be fulfilled. 2,000 years have passed and history did not reach its climax as they expected. They were not, in fact, living in the last days before the climax of history. It did not occur in their lifetime and it has not occurred in the 2,000 years since.

As time passed and their hopes were not fulfilled as they expected, we might wonder why the movement did not simply collapse, as many other movements with such failed expectations have done. Obviously, there was more holding it together than the belief that they were living in the last days. Over time the hope of the resurrection and of the last judgment was pushed out into the distant future where they have remained in Christian faith right through to today, where they are now almost just an appendix to faith rather than being at its center.

Christian faith survived because at its heart was something much more important than expectations about timing. We see this well illustrated in the Gospel according to John, which portrays Jesus as offering "eternal life" to people already during his ministry. Clearly this was not just a promise about the future, but a promise about the present. That Gospel speaks about eternal life as a quality of life in relationship to God rather than a statement about quantity of life. Hence the images it uses to depict eternal life: bread, water, light, life.

According to the Fourth Gospel, eternal life is life in relationship with God mediated through Jesus and that life is to be had already in the here and now and would last even beyond death. The Gospel writer is quite daring in depicting the coming to faith and the receiving of that life as the moment when a person is born from above (3:3–5) or even more dramatically: their moment of resurrection. Instead of confining talk of resurrection to the end of time, the author says in effect that in receiving such life people have already been resurrected. He even says that people have already passed through judgment (5:24).

Such creative thought did not abandon the traditional ideas of a future general resurrection and a day of judgment, but it changed the focus to life in relationship with God in the present. That relationship began in faith and would continue even beyond death.

Another important element in this development was the belief that after death people were not in fact reduced to a half-life, a kind of sleeping reality, as they waited for resurrection. Already some fellow Jews had begun to move away from this older view. After death people will, they came to believe, have conscious existence. They even speculated that at death they would already be judged and be brought into God's presence or sent off to hell.

The parable of the rich man and Lazarus in Luke's Gospel assumes this pattern, for it depicts Lazarus in heaven and the rich man in hell (Luke 16:19–31). This makes sense of Luke's creative embellishment of the story of Jesus' crucifixion where he imagines one of those crucified with Jesus repenting and being told that that day he would join Jesus in paradise (23:43). The Gospel according to John certainly assumes that after his death and resurrection Jesus would be returning to God's glory and that believers on their death would follow him there (12:25–26). Thus, in his prayer Jesus prays that they might join him there (17:24).

Even Paul, who still uses the language of people falling asleep to describe death (1 Cor 15:20), can write of dying and being with Christ as much more than a sleepy awareness, but rather as something to which he looks forward (Phil 1:21–26). The effect of believing in hope for a quality of life already after death further marginalized the notion of a day of resurrection and judgment as traditionally understood, making it almost redundant, though for most it did not go that far.

Embracing Hope Today

When we contemplate what hope means for us, compared with what it meant for John the Baptist, Jesus, and the early believers, we find some help by observing these developments. In the light of them we cannot avoid making choices. They are to embrace some aspects and respectfully to leave some others behind, not least the belief that the end of history would occur in the first century CE!

While we are no longer able to embrace the belief in a macro-change to be brought about by God in the first century CE, we can still embrace what that vision entailed with regard to its substance. Using Jesus' ministry as a model, as preserved in the anecdotes and sayings of Jesus, we, too, can embrace the larger vision of good news for the poor that he proclaimed. Indeed, we, too, can reflect on the imagery of the great feast where love offers a place for all. Our highly stylized liturgy of the Eucharist remains a significant starting point for embracing such hope. It foreshadows the vision that we espouse.

For us, that vision sets our agenda. It is, however, no longer something we expect to be brought about by a sudden divine intervention as they imagined. It is rather a vision of what we can see as a possibility as we seek to encourage people to be open to God's life and love in our community and our world.

They expanded that vision to include not only a renewal of humanity but also a renewal of creation, indeed a new heaven and new earth, and sometimes as a reestablishment of paradise as at the beginning. We see this in the final chapter of the book of Revelation. Our hopes embrace commitment to responding to God's love also for creation as well as for all people, including future generations and so inspire us to embrace the challenges of climate change.

As we reconfigure our approach to hope, retaining the central substance of theirs, but not their notions of timing and manner of its achievement, we can also gain value by holding onto what enabled their faith to survive after their expectations failed to be realized. This means that like the author of the Fourth Gospel we can put our focus above all on life in relationship with God and in effect locate our hope not in some future event and intervention, let alone its timing, but in the being of God.

Clearly, hope generated imagination and the result was a range of traditional images, whether of heavenly mansions and golden streets or abundance and fertility in a renewed paradise. People also imagined resurrection of the righteous who would shine like stars or like the transfigured Jesus foreshadowing resurrection existence. Perhaps it now makes more sense to focus simply on one detail: God and that God is love. For some people this detail about the future is all that is needed. We go to be in the hands of God. It is very human to want to know more and want to be able to explain more.

While that may well suffice for individual hope, we need much more in relation to the way we appropriate Jesus' macro-vision. That needs to be concrete and informed as we seek to understand what it means in reality to be a just and caring society that is inclusive and to care for the world and its future inhabitants and to see that challenge as our way of sharing God's being and priorities. That means being "good news for the poor," a hope that has proved very difficult to sustain and easy to subvert with spiritualities that in effect undermine it. In the next chapter we shall explore why it matters and how it might be sustained.

Reflection: How can we ensure that hope is more than just a set of goals to work towards? What energizes and enables hope?

6

What Happened to
"Good News for the Poor"?

Blessed are you poor, if you try to get a job and work hard.
Blessed are you who are hungry now;
it is really important that you eat healthy food.
Blessed are you who weep now;
don't worry, you'll feel better in the morning.
(with apologies to Luke 6:20–21)

In Jesus' world if you were sick, you would become poor. If you had a disability, you would be poor. If you were poor, you would need to beg. If you were lucky, someone, perhaps even your local synagogue community, might give you some temporary help following biblical injunctions to care for the poor. In Galilee, blessed with fertile soil for grain growing, some fared very well, but others were at the bottom of society's heap.

I find it very difficult, living in a prosperous country like Australia, to keep in touch with what life means for those both within Australia and beyond it who struggle to make it and who live below the poverty line. I see it as an effort I need to make if I am going to have any idea of what Jesus' priorities were and have any chance of being a decent human being. I am surrounded often by very different agendas—in the community and sometimes in the church. The more carefully I seek to reconstruct the history through detailed academic research, the more I am confronted with what is a present reality for so many. It is hard for "Good News for the Poor" to survive in our world, but, alas, also in the church. This chapter starts by looking at the traps of poverty that confronted Jesus.

Little was likely to change. Rome's agents, Herod Antipas in Galilee, Philip across the Jordan, and Rome's "prefect" in Judea held sway and demanded their share of anything you produced, managed by their hired tax and toll collectors. If you were poor, you would often have no employment or at best you might be hired as a day laborer. And if you were employed on a permanent basis, you would be working for a landlord. You would usually be a tenant with a small plot of land. Many of Jesus' parables are a window onto this reality. Your landlord would also want his share and in return offer you some security that helped you survive and held you in dependency.

Jesus and Good News for the Poor

When Jesus called some to leave these secure settings and led a group of such followers around Galilee, it was a risky undertaking and also a protest against this tight system that trapped people in poverty and secured people in wealth. There was not such desperate poverty that the group could not survive. They could claim hospitality from those who responded to their message. But they lived from day to day, as Jesus put it, trusting like birds and the lilies of the field that their settings would support them (Matt 6:25–34; Luke 12:22–32).

The call to follow Jesus really did mean for some leaving the security of family and of work if they had it (Mark 1:16–20; 10:16–22; Matt 8:19–22; Luke 9:57–62). For others to follow Jesus meant staying put but embracing his radical hope for change and his radical lifestyle in seeking already to bring change (Mark 5:18–20).

As we have seen in previous chapters, Jesus' vision of change was big. It entailed not only the micro-change that he and his followers were able to enact around Galilee, but also macro-change that included a new way of being community and being governed with God as the ruler, the kingdom of God. It was a hope not just for individual relief from poverty but also for the people as a whole, sometimes described collectively as "the poor."

Some of Jesus' sayings are rich with imagery relating to the nation. Luke has him promise his disciples:

> You are those who have stood by me in my trials; 29and I confer on you, just as my Father has conferred on me, a kingdom, 30so

that you may eat and drink at my table in my kingdom, and you will sit on thrones judging the twelve tribes of Israel. (22:28–30)

Luke on Good News for the Poor

Of all the Gospels, Luke most emphasizes this corporate dimension of hope for Israel as a whole. Taking Mark as his frame and adding further material to which both he and Matthew had access, Luke introduces his Gospel with scenes that closely tie faith to Israel and its hopes. In part he is setting John the Baptist and Jesus side by side.

An angel tells Zechariah that his wife, Elizabeth, would bear a son. They would name him John, and he would be great (1:13–17). Similarly, an angel tells Mary that she will bear a son. They would name him Jesus and he would be great (1:30–33). Then Mary and Elizabeth meet (1:39–45). John is born and was circumcised and grew and was filled with the Spirit (1:57–59, 80). Similarly, Jesus was born and was circumcised and grew in wisdom and favor with God and with people (2:1–40). Of course, despite the parallels, there was a difference: John was a prophet. Jesus was the Son of God.

Luke was doing more, however, than comparing and contrasting John and Jesus. At significant points in the story he has the lead characters give voice to Israel's hope. Thus Zechariah blessed God who was about to liberate the people, raising up a "horn of salvation . . . in the house of his servant David," to save them from their enemies and guide them into the way of peace (1:68–79). Similarly Mary's song, known as the Magnificat, hails God as the one who has brought down the powerful from their thrones and lifted up the lowly, . . . filled the hungry with good things, and sent the rich empty away . . . helped his servant Israel, in remembrance of his mercy (1:46–55). These sound like statements about the past, but really they are statements about what was about to happen in the future.

Luke portrays other characters, too, as sharing the same hope. Thus, he describes the "righteous and godly" man, Simeon, waiting for "the consolation of Israel" (2:25–35) and has Anna, the prophetess, speaking about Jesus to those who were "looking for Jerusalem's liberation" (2:36–38).

In producing these scenes of people longing for Israel's liberation, Luke was not engaged in decoration. Nor was he about to use such images in a spiritualizing way to say that Jesus came to bring people forgiveness from their sins, a different kind of liberation, so that these scenes and the hopes they express have only symbolic value. On the contrary, Luke continues the theme of these hopes. He describes Joseph of Arimathea as similarly a "good and righteous man" who was looking for the kingdom of God (23:50–54). Luke portrays Jesus, himself, as addressing the people of Jerusalem, encouraging them to lift up their heads when the great disasters of the sacking of Jerusalem would come upon them because they would then soon see him coming to them (21:28).

The theme continues in the story of the disciples on the Emmaus Road who in conversation with Jesus *incognito* bemoan the fact that they had hoped that "he was going to liberate Israel" (24:19–21). Jesus' response was not to tell them to give up such hopes, but to challenge them to see that his suffering was also part of what was to be expected (24:25–27). Similarly, in the scene at the beginning of the book of Acts where Jesus ascends from them, the disciples ask him: "Will you at this time restore the kingdom to Israel?" (1:6). Again, Jesus does not reprimand them and tell them to abandon such hopes, but simply explains that the timing is a matter for God and that in the meantime they should go out into the world to spread his message (1:7–8).

In one of Peter's speeches to the crowds in Jerusalem he exhorts them:

> Repent therefore, and turn to God so that your sins may be wiped out, 20so that times of refreshing may come from the presence of the Lord, and that he may send the Messiah appointed for you, that is, Jesus, 21who must remain in heaven until the time of universal restoration that God announced long ago through his holy prophets. (3:19–21)

For Luke, writing probably some 50 years after Jesus, the hope of the restoration of Israel, of good news for the poor, was still very much alive. The notion of future hope as beginning with Christ's return to Jerusalem and there setting up God's kingdom of compassion and peace survived well into the second century, especially among Jewish believers. The church father, Justin Martyr, in the mid-second century expounded such hope. "Good news for the poor" was alive and well.

Problems with Hope for "The Poor"

It was not so straightforward to speak about good news for the poor out in the wider world. And here there were two problems. One was that as time went on the hope failed to materialize. The other was that, while such a hope meant something to Jews, it had less relevance for other peoples. At its best, such hope, as we have seen, had a place for other peoples. They would join Israel, live in peace alongside Israel, learning God's law. They would be like the birds finding shelter under the mustard bush (Mark 4:30–32).

It would have been of limited appeal, for instance, for the inhabitants of Antioch or Rome to be told that the coming of a Jewish Messiah and his establishment of a Jerusalem-based kingdom was good news for them. Very early, "Christ," the Greek translation of the Hebrew "Messiah," which meant "Anointed," lost its significance in such circles and came to be little more than the equivalent of a surname. So it was as though he was Jesus Christ, son of Mr. and Mrs. Christ.

In non-Jewish contexts the gospel would not cut through if it was so much tied to Israel. It needed to focus on the universal dimension if it was to be seen and heard as relevant to people outside Israel. The focus might still have been liberation from the Romans, but the preferred focus was liberation from the prospects of condemnation at the last judgment, as we have seen in earlier chapters. That went hand in hand, therefore, with seeing the danger not as Rome now but as eternal punishment in hell. The benefit was accordingly not so much social change now as the prospect of heaven, where suffering and pain and poverty would be no more. Then the hope of God's reign came to mean the hope of heaven. Heaven's kingdom, as Matthew preferred to put it, when still speaking of God's reign on earth, came to be taken literally as God's reign in the heavens, and more especially as a place, heaven.

The transition was by no means simple. Good news for the poor persisted and continued to inform these changing thoughts. Among those with a strongly Jewish faith, like Paul, good news for the poor came to be extended to non-Jews as well as Jews when they turned to Israel's God and responded to the free offer of a relationship with God brought to them by Jesus. By being incorporated into Israel, like being grafted into an existing tree, these outsiders became insiders and so what was promised to Israel also came to be promised to those who were once outsiders. He uses the illustration of grafting in writing to the Romans (11:17).

The shift here is subtle. What Jesus offered to all Israel, preachers like Paul continued to offer to Israel, but now with two qualifications. Firstly, outsiders, non-Jews, needed to become insiders, to join the people of God, and, secondly, in any case the Israel of God was at best those Jews who recognized and acclaimed Jesus as the Christ. "The poor," used broadly to refer to all Israel, became therefore redefined to refer to the faithful Israel plus the newcomers. Paul could not, however, bring himself to believe that the rest of Israel, who has not responded to the gospel, would now be damned because he could not believe God would give them up. He comforts himself with the faith in what he calls a mystery: somehow God will include them too (Rom 11:29–32).

The Poor and the Church

When we look to see how the early believers responded to issues of poverty, we find that their focus was primarily on caring for fellow believers. Famously, Paul's innovative expansion of the gospel to non-Jews won approval from the apostles in part on the basis that he would remember the poor (Gal 2:10). Indeed, he did; and made a collection from among his churches for the poor among the saints in Jerusalem (1 Cor 8—9). These may well have been the survivors of some of those who had left homes and sold property and had settled in Jerusalem to await the promised end, but whose lifestyle proved unsustainable.

Paul also challenges the churches in Corinth over the neglect of the poor, especially in the context of the fellowship meals, which along with the Eucharist formed part of their weekly gatherings (1 Cor 11:17–34). Those who were forced to come late missed out. Paul knew that the Eucharist was a foreshadowing of the great feast when all would have a place and plenty of food, so to have it conducted in a way that deprived some members failed to discern what being the body of Christ meant and what partaking of the one bread symbolized.

In Paul's Christian communities, as far as we can see, the focus remained primarily on helping the poor among their members. There is no mention of extending the concern about poverty to the wider community. In the Gospel according to John, we have an indirect reference to money held by Judas, which in part was intended to be used to bring relief to the poor (13:29). Apart from that, here, too, the focus is on loving one another as members of the believing community.

In the first letter of John, written by a different hand, but within the same circles of believers, we find strong emphasis on loving one another. This is not about being nice and friendly, as these words have often been watered down to become in our world, but had to include caring about other people's survival. The author declares:

> How does God's love abide in anyone who has the world's goods
> and sees a brother or sister in need and yet refuses help? (3:17)

Luke on the Rich and the Poor

To return to Luke, the book of Acts, his second volume, portrays the first believers in Jerusalem as a tight knit community, where, like some other Jewish movements of the time, they sold up property and shared resources (2:42–47; 4:32–37). This was even to the extent of deeming those who did not do so, or just pretended to share, worthy of the death penalty (5:1–11), a violent end. Luke may have been idealizing and reflecting some of the idealists of his time, because such divestment of property and communal living was not the practice elsewhere and would not be sustainable over time.

Luke must have been writing in a context where the churches, namely the house groups, likely to be listening to his works, included both rich and poor. In embracing the hope of major change, leading to liberation for Israel and the reign of God as compassionate and inclusive, Luke shows himself very aware that this also needed to shape people's behavior in the present.

For Luke "salvation" had to mean a change of attitude towards the poor. He cites the example of Zacchaeus whose response to Jesus is to declare that he is willing to restore fourfold what he has ripped off from other people, to which Jesus comments, "Today salvation has come to this house. For he, too, is a son of Abraham" (19:9). Salvation shows itself in such commitment. Similarly Jewish is the context of the parable about the rich man and Lazarus, where Lazarus find himself in the bosom of Abraham (16:19–31). Even more directly, Luke brings a set of woes to match the blessings pronounced on the poor, hungry, and those who weep.

> But woe to you who are rich, for you have received your consolation.
> Woe to you who are full now, for you will be hungry.
> Woe to you who are laughing now, for you will mourn and weep.
> (6:24–25)

What Happened to Good News for the Poor?

What, then, happened to good news for the poor? It survived in the expectation held by Luke, for instance, that one day God's kingdom would be set up in Jerusalem with Jesus as Messiah, ruling on God's behalf, when all the promises entailed in Jesus' vision of the kingdom would come true. They did not take the option we embrace, of taking what Jesus promised to his people, Israel, and extending it to a commitment to bring hope for the poor among all peoples. At most they included non-Jews in the promise only when they joined the people of God and so qualified to share its promises. Care for the poor outside the believing communities does not feature otherwise, though one should not assume it did not occur at all.

For many, however, the delay in fulfillment and the particular Jewishness of the expectation as originally formulated gave way to seeing its fulfillment not as taking place in an earthly setting, let alone centered on Judea and Jerusalem. Instead its fulfillment would now be in the heavenly world, in heaven. Continuing pessimism and vulnerability to disease and suffering of all sorts helped develop an imagining of hope as release from living in this world and this became a dominant focus for centuries. Some went so far as to deem this world the creation of a deviant divine being bent on meanness and not God at all. In the main, most believing communities rejected that view and held to belief in God as creator, but clearly for many the prospect of positive change in this world was very unlikely.

One solution where life was so grim, as it was for many people, was, of course, to locate hope in another world and another time: the heavenly world. Another was to spiritualize all such hopes for change and retreat into the peace one might find in one's inner world. Sometimes these reconfigurings of hope led to a giving up of hope and commitment to good news for the poor. Salvation was about the soul and the afterlife.

Tragically this sometimes meant that those who cried out for change and relief in this world were comforted or confronted with the message: just wait for the world to come or find your inner fulfillment. Don't bother yourself about seeking change in the here and now. It suited governments and dictators to encourage such religion, because it silenced their concerns. A similar logic informs those who dismiss concerns with climate change on the basis that there will one day be a new heaven and a new earth and who find allies in businesses that fear any action to deal with it might diminish their profits.

Love and the good news it generates have remarkable ways of surviving. In centuries after Christianity's beginnings, monastic movements developed, which were able to combine hope in heaven beyond and hope in an inner peace with a firm commitment in word and action to becoming good news for the poor in their world. They had in common with Jesus that, just as he saw all his compatriots as belonging to Israel, so they could see all theirs as Christian, especially when it became the dominant religion of their world. This is not the case in our world, but we have learned that God's compassion and the promise of good news for the poor cannot be confined to those who see themselves as God's people. An understanding of God as loving breaks through these traditional barriers.

In our times we see that even those sections of Protestant Christianity that once were almost solely focused on rescuing people from hell have embraced the commission also to be good news for the poor and to act for social justice in our own world. And others for whom faith has become redefined in terms of personal well-being and counseling support to help people cope with life, have often also opened up to the realization that individual well-being is only part of the gospel. The gospel must always be about the bigger picture including the structures of government and society that hold people back in poverty, disadvantage, and discrimination. Helping people adjust to these is an inadequate half-answer.

The same is to be observed often in those Christian communities where the focus appears to be the feelings of exhilaration associated with group celebration and hyperventilation. Paul challenged the Corinthians groups obsessed with being carried away as they had been in their pagan days but now by what they claimed was the work of the Spirit. He did not ask them to deny their experiences, their gifts of the Spirit, but he made it clear that the more excellent way was to locate the Spirit where love, its fruit, was evident. He expressed his claim above all in his eloquent chapter on love (1 Cor 13).

Good News for the Poor Today

At their best, churches are not only places where people support and love one another but also places that generate acts of love and compassion in their world. They learn to speak the language of Jesus and walk in his ways and, indeed, when they do, they find many other travelers on the way. Such travelers may have also had to work their way through their own religious traditions to recognize distractions and to treasure the core values that make for a healthier society.

"Good news for the poor" is just as much needed to today as it was in the world of Jesus. Today we find very mixed motives among those concerned with poverty. For business, it is not in their interests to have people being poor. They will have no money to spend on their products. As millions move from poverty into the middle class in India and China on a scale undreamt of, industry thrives, and employment grows. World poverty, measured by those who live on less than a dollar a day, has all but halved in recent decades. The vision of good news for the poor is paradoxically being promoted very effectively by those who primarily pursue self-interest. Even then, however, we need to recognize that some companies make caring for their workforce and for people part of what they want to be and be known for. This is not to be despised.

The weakness in such development is that it often leaves behind those unable to be productive in the workforce through age or disability. Concern about good news for the poor needs to be more all-encompassing and not motivated by how that might profit us, much as we need to welcome the changes brought about.

There have been many ways of removing good news for the poor from the center of the gospel. It was in danger of not surviving or of being confined to care for members. We have needed to delimit the narrowed focus that was dominant in Christian beginnings and let love be its limitless self, lifting our eyes to see all in need and opening our ears to hear all who cry, not just believers. Then we need to use our brains to work out how most effectively to change structures, implement programs, and provide resources that will help people help themselves out of poverty's traps. That includes making sure there are protections against exploitation, discrimination, and greed. But ultimately it is about letting God and God's love take us beyond rules and protections to willing engagement and determined initiatives to effect change.

The key question remains for those who would claim Christian identity: are we good news for the poor? If not, we have embraced something other than the gospel of Jesus.

Reflection: What does it mean to be Good News for the Poor in your world?

SECTION C

Love: What Can Love Do?

7

Do We Still Need the Law?

Do not think I have come to abolish the law or the prophets. I have not come to abolish them but to replace them with a better righteousness. For until I came, not a jot or stroke was to pass from the law; it was all to be done. But now anyone continuing to teach even the least significant of its commandments shall be called least in the kingdom of heaven. For unless your righteousness is much better than that of the scribes and the Pharisees, you will not enter the kingdom of heaven. You have heard that those of old were told to keep the commandments, but I now say something very different and more profound. (with apologies to Matt 5:17–21)

THIS RADICALLY CHANGES THE statement that Matthew has Jesus pronounce at the beginning of his teaching on the Sermon on the Mount, but, strangely, it fits the way many people interpreted his words.

An extreme form of this thinking arose in the latter decades of the twentieth century where movements arose, including in the church that declared, "If it feels right do it!" While this loosened the bonds of people who had lived with a form of Christianity that was full of "oughts" and "don'ts," it also let loose behaviors where people turned off their brains. The result in many instances was not just self-indulgence but also sexual promiscuity and abuse. I can remember the grounding wisdom that countered: the most important sexual organ is the brain.

It was also in these decades that historical research came to a much more nuanced understanding of the context of New Testament writings, especially their Jewish context, rediscovered not least because of the stimulus of finding the ancient library of Jewish literature in caves by the Dead Sea Seaand because the Holocaust exposed the legacy of prejudice. New Testament writings were not all the same and differed in their approach to the biblical law (in effect the major part of the Jewish Scriptures). It enabled us to see that Matthew needed to be read differently from what had been the common understanding reflected in the reformulation presented above.

Biblical law, sometimes described as the law of Moses, the Torah, refers to the commandments and instructions set out above all in the first five books of the Old Testament, sometimes called the books of Moses. It was and is foundational for Jewish life and is viewed as God's gift to Israel to enable it to remain faithful to the covenant with God. It includes but is more than the Ten Commandments and includes directions for many aspects of daily life as well for observation of ritual purity, what is clean and unclean, and the basic provisions necessary for the structure and running of the temple and its rituals.

What Jesus Really Said About the Law According to Matthew

The original words in Matthew begin by saying:

> Do not think I have come to abolish the law or the prophets. I have not come to abolish but to fulfill. (5:17)

Fulfilling the requirements and the conditions for something does not usually mean setting them aside, let alone replacing them. It means something more like upholding them. This is true of its meaning here and makes sense of what follows, which declares:

> For until heaven and earth pass away not one jot or stroke will pass from the law, until all is done* (5:18).

That is another way of saying that the law remains permanently in effect. This, in turn, also makes sense of the warning that follows:

> Whoever sets aside one of the least of these commandments and teaches people to do so shall be called least in the kingdom of heaven; and who keeps them and teaches people to do so will be called great. For I tell you, unless your righteousness exceeds that of the scribes and Pharisees, you will never enter the kingdom of heaven.* (5:19–20)

The greater righteousness in the verse that follows is not about keeping a different law but keeping the same law as set out in the Scriptures more faithfully and strictly.

When Matthew then has Jesus comment on six aspects of the law in 5:21–48, he contrasts what people heard in the past with what it really meant. Thus, "Don't murder" also implied, "Don't have murderous, hateful thoughts and attitudes" and he applied the same to the command not to commit adultery.

Matthew on the Law

The author of the Gospel according to Matthew was writing some 50 years after the time of Jesus and never gave us his name. All the Gospels are in fact anonymous. His Gospel came to be associated with the disciple, Matthew, possibly because it was written in an area where that disciple had been active. We call the author Matthew for short. It seems he was writing in a setting that was strongly Jewish, with local communal government in the hands of Jewish leaders (23:2–3). He was very careful in the way he used Mark, his main source, and other material, to which Luke independently also had access. When Matthew rewrites Mark, he does so in a way that gives special emphasis to the law in Jesus' teaching.

One of the ways he does this is by grouping nearly all the sayings of Jesus into five main clusters, which he portrays as speeches of Jesus. He may well have done so deliberately to echo the fact that the law consisted of the five so-called books of Moses, Genesis to Deuteronomy.

He has Jesus give the opening speech up on a mountain. For people listening to Matthew's story of Jesus, the symbolism would have been obvious. Jesus goes up a mountain to teach about God's law, just as Moses had gone up Mt. Sinai to receive God's law.

This follows the opening chapters of his Gospel where he portrays Jesus as the judge to come, announced by John the Baptist. In his opening speech, Jesus as the judge to come announces the basis upon which people will be judged. They will be judged on the basis of how they have kept God's law and in particular whether they kept it in the way that Jesus taught it should be kept.

If, therefore, we ask Matthew whether we still need the law, the answer is straightforward: it is essential. Elsewhere he has Jesus underline that people will be judged on the basis of their behavior (16:27). Every speech of Jesus in Matthew's Gospel ends with warnings about the judgment. His final speech uses the image of the day of judgment as the act of separating sheep from goats (25:31–46). What would make the difference? Behavior: whether people showed love and care for those in need in their community.

There were, however, different approaches to keeping the law. For some, the emphasis was on strict observance of every detail equally and especially of such requirements as observing food laws, keeping oneself "clean" in a ritual sense by ceremonial washings, and not working on the sabbath. These belong to the jots and strokes that Matthew also assumes all should keep. They are not seen as burdensome. He even insists that people should tithe the herbs they harvest, going further than what the law actually required, but he does so only after first stating what he saw as the priorities of Jesus. Not all commands are of equal weight.

> Woe to you, scribes and Pharisees, hypocrites! For you tithe mint, dill, and cumin, and have neglected the weightier matters of the law: justice and mercy and faith. It is these you ought to have practiced without neglecting the others. (23:23)

Matthew depicts Jesus as advocating a very different approach from that of the scribes and Pharisees, as he portrays it. Matthew may well be doing so against the background of conflict in his own day between his community of Jewish believers and those who had come to dominate leadership of the synagogues. Synagogues were re-establishing themselves in the 80s after the debacle of the fall of Jerusalem and destruction of the temple in 70 CE. Matthew may or may not be accurate about their views. In conflicts it is easy to be misrepresented.

The priorities Matthew highlights are reflected in what he presents as Jesus' concerns in keeping the law: "justice and mercy and faith." Similarly, the Sermon on the Mount puts the emphasis upon moral rather than ritual issues, especially in 5:21–48. Hence his focus on the evil of harbored anger and adulterous attitudes in expounding the prohibition of murder and adultery (5:21–30). On divorce and oaths (5:31–37) he is also much stricter than the letter of the law demands and his focus on loving enemies and not engaging in retaliation (5:38–48) reflects the best of Jewish and Old Testament teaching.

It is, of course, possible to quote texts from the Old Testament—indeed from the New—that reflect hatred of enemies and imply retaliation and vengeance, but Matthew typically has Jesus emphasize loving God and loving one's neighbor.

When the Pharisees heard that he had silenced the Sadducees, they gathered together, and one of them, a lawyer, asked him a question to test him. "Teacher, which commandment in the law is the greatest?" He said to him, "'You shall love the Lord your God with all your heart, and with all your soul, and with all your mind.' This is the greatest and first commandment. And a second is like it: 'You shall love your neighbour as yourself.' On these two commandments hang all the law and the prophets." (22:34–40)

In everything do to others as you would have them do to you; for this is the law and the prophets. (7:12)

Behind Matthew: Mark and Jesus

Matthew's stance is, to that extent, a continuation of Jesus' own stance. Fifty years earlier Jesus, too, had conflict with his contemporaries, especially those who disapproved of his healing people on the sabbath and his mixing with tax collectors and other noted sinners. In the sprinkling of anecdotes that have survived, preserved in their earliest form in Mark's Gospel, we find Jesus responding to such criticism in telling ways.

In response to the criticism about bad company, Jesus simply declares: "The sick need a doctor not the well"* (Mark 2:17). In other words, his focus was human need, not how to protect himself from ritual impurity or moral contamination. When they quibbled about his right to declare to the paralyzed man that his sins were forgiven, he replied: "What is easier: to say to the paralyzed man, 'Your sins are forgiven' or to say 'Take up your bed and walk'"* (2:9). And when they criticized his disciples for plucking and eating grain on the sabbath, Jesus retorted: "The sabbath was made for people; not people for the sabbath"* (Mark 2:27).

Jesus, too, upheld the law, but in a way that put love at the center as the basis for deciding what should have priority in interpreting it. He reflects the best Jewish thought of his time when he summarized the law as loving God and loving one's neighbor (Mark 12:28–31).

Mark brings a story about a rich man who wants to know how to obtain eternal life (10:17–22). Jesus' answer is clear: he needs to keep the law, which Jesus then typically spells out by focusing on the moral commandments, do not kill, do not commit adultery, do not steal, do not give false testimony, do not defraud, honor your father and mother.

The man claims to have kept all of these and wins Jesus' admiration, but then Jesus tests him to see if he really grasps what is at the heart of the law, challenging him to sell up his possessions and give the proceeds to the poor. The man could not contemplate engaging in such generosity and turned away disappointed. In the story Jesus is shown as exposing the man as having little room in his mind for love for others, and so not willing to contemplate Jesus' challenge. The message is clear: you gain eternal life by sharing God's eternal life and love in keeping at least the moral commandments of the law. That was how, Mark argued, Jesus interpreted the law. We will return to Mark's stance on the law, but first we turn to Luke.

Luke and the Law

Matthew's approach, 50 years after Jesus, stands in continuity with Jesus' approach, as does Luke's approach. They both shared the same source of sayings, so that in Luke we read:

> It is easier for heaven and earth to pass away, than for one stroke of
> a letter in the law to be dropped. (16:17)

This, too, like Matthew's statement in the Sermon on the Mount, has been misread to indicate the opposite of what it intends. For Luke introduces it with the words:

> The law and the prophets were in effect until John came; since then
> the good news of the kingdom of God is proclaimed, and everyone
> acts against it by force.* (16:16)

The misreading proposes that Luke means that the law and the prophets ceased to be in effect after John the Baptist and have been replaced since then with the good news. On the contrary, rather, as in Matthew, Luke is saying that just as the law and the prophets faced resistance, so now the gospel, added to them, is also facing fierce resistance.

The statement about not even a stroke of the letter being dropped is not to indicate that now the law should be dropped, but rather that not even a stroke of it should be dropped, just as in Matthew. Luke then reinforces this by pointing to Jesus' very strict teaching about divorce in the verse that follows.

Luke is consistent. He even portrays Paul as remaining totally obedient to the law, depicting him as wrongly criticized for not doing so (Acts

21:21). For Luke the law is permanent, but there are exceptions authorized by God. He reports a major exception that arose in the context of the spread of the faith into the wider Roman empire where people other than Jews (gentiles) heard and responded to the gospel and sought to join the movement. He relates it to Paul's initiatives, in particular, but in the first instance to Peter.

Gentiles were joining the faith community. Jews in the Jesus movement on the basis of the law set out in Genesis 17, insisted that male gentiles who joined the community were to be circumcised.

> Throughout your generations every male among you shall be circumcised when he is eight days old, including the slave born in your house and the one bought with your money from any foreigner who is not of your offspring. 13Both the slave born in your house and the one bought with your money must be circumcised. So shall my covenant be in your flesh an everlasting covenant. 14Any uncircumcised male who is not circumcised in the flesh of his foreskin shall be cut off from his people; he has broken my covenant. (Gen 17:12–14)

To them this was incontrovertible. The biblical law demanded it. It should have, therefore, been straightforward. Gentile male believers should have been circumcised. Perhaps because there were so many of them—for many gentiles attended Jewish synagogues—and more probably out of a rational sense of compassion, the majority of believers came to the belief that God would not insist on this commandment being kept. They were following the priorities set by Jesus but going a step further to say, we set this requirement aside permanently, much to the relief of the foreign men.

There was, of course, stiff resistance from some believers. How could you set God's law aside? They argued much like fundamentalists in our own time that there can be no exceptions when it comes to keeping the commandments.

Luke explains how the change occurred and justifies it by telling a story about Peter (Acts 10:9–16). Peter has a vision of seeing animals and being told by a heavenly voice that he should kill and eat some of them. The animals he saw were, however, the ones the law forbids Jews to eat and so Peter protests. The heavenly voice then rebukes Peter with the words: "Do not call what God has purified unclean" (2:15).

Luke may be using a story about a vision whose point was to lift the restrictions on what meat one could eat, making it easier for Jews and non-Jews to eat together, but this is not how Luke uses it. He uses it to have God persuade Peter not to see gentiles as impure or unclean. The outcome is that Peter goes to a gentile's house, preaches, and wins gentiles to become followers of Jesus—but did not circumcise them (Acts 10:17–48).

Luke reports that as a result the leaders of the movement, including Jesus' brother James, the leader of the Jerusalem church, Peter, and the other apostles, but also Paul and Barnabas, came together to discuss what they should do about gentiles (Acts 15). The extensive and successful missions of Barnabas and Paul had raised the issue on a grand scale, and it needed resolution. Some insisted gentiles be circumcised.

The so-called Jerusalem Council resolved not to require that gentiles be circumcised and, apart from that, that gentiles should observe only some minimal laws, namely about abstaining from eating idol meat, strangled and blood products, and sexual immorality, some reflecting biblical law. For Jewish believers the law remained totally intact and Luke, accordingly, portrays Paul and others as observant, aside from this exception. The fundamentalists among the believers still strongly disagreed, and we even find them, for instance, conducting their own missions among faith communities that Paul had established in Galatia, in order to bring them into line with their thinking (Gal 1:6–9; 5:7–12).

Paul and the Law

Luke was writing some 20–30 years after Paul was active and, while they may have met and even spent some time together, it is clear that Luke's memory of events and of Paul, himself, was not always accurate, even though Luke portrays Paul as a hero. Luke appears to have smoothed over some of the conflicts that Paul had, as well as reflecting some confusion, possibly in his sources, for instance, about how many times Paul went back to Jerusalem.

Fortunately, we have at least seven of Paul's own letters, as well as another six written in his name by those who sought to call on his authority and perpetuate his approach. Paul took the approach that circumcision was unnecessary but went further. He gives us his own account of the Jerusalem Council in his letter to the Galatians (2:1–10) and in addition reports a subsequent conflict that arose in Antioch, which is very revealing (2:11–14).

There, Paul and Barnabas, as well as Peter, had adopted the practice of sharing together in common meals with the community of faith, which included both Jews and gentiles. What seemed a very natural outcome of the inclusion of both was thrown into confusion when some of the Jerusalem believers from James' church came to Antioch. They argued that such fellowship ran contrary to God's law, at least in the sense that traditionally Jews might visit gentile homes occasionally but should not do so on a regular basis because of the assumed dangers of contamination.

Astonishingly, Peter, but also Paul's mission partner, Barnabas, complied and withdrew. Paul makes it clear that he was outraged. He saw this as a contradiction of what his gospel proclaimed, namely that God's grace and forgiveness was just as freely available to non-Jews as it was to Jews. This radical love on God's part opened the door unconditionally to both. There was no requirement as he saw it that they first agree to observe the law. They were all saved by God's goodness and grace and this was to be embraced by simply believing and entering the relationship on offer. Their loyalty henceforth was not to the law but to Christ.

Paul was therefore at loggerheads not only with the fundamentalist believers who kept insisting on circumcision and total observance of biblical law, but also with those who later, like Luke, insisted on full observance of the law apart from a few exceptions such as circumcision. Paul was forced onto the defensive, but that stimulated him to offer a profound account of the gospel as he understood it, which has remained influential to our own day.

Paul Explains His View to the Romans

His clearest explanation is in his letter to the Romans, where he is preparing to visit them and so wants to explain what he has been preaching and defend it against the criticism of it, which will have reached the ears of the Roman Christians. By saying that God offers all a relationship of forgiveness and love without first insisting that they keep and remain committed to keeping the law, he did not mean, he argued, that he was advocating that people simply become lawless and do as they like, as some alleged (3:5–8).

And he was certainly not advocating that people sin as much as they can to gain as much forgiveness as possible (6:1–2). And he was not, he insisted, betraying his own Jewish people by suggesting that God had given up on them (3:1–4; 9—11).

Paul makes his case for treating Jews and gentiles equally by arguing that they are both in need of God and God's forgiveness (3:9–23). Those in Rome listening to his letter being read would have surely welcomed his sample account of the pagan world's evil in 1:18–28, which focused on same-sex relations as typical of what they all condemned as contrary to nature and God's creation, but would then have been challenged by what follows.

For Paul goes on to argue that his fellow Jews are no better than people of the pagan world, because while they know God's laws, they do not keep them (2:1–11). Gentiles have an inner sense of right and wrong and fail (2:12–16). Jews have written laws and also fail. Their being circumcised does not make up for this (2:25–29). Using an image from his Jewish heritage (Deut 10:16; 30:6), he insists that circumcision of the heart or mind is what really counts.

Accordingly, all have sinned and, like Adam, fallen short of the glory God intended for them (3:23). If we push this declaration statistically, this would imply that every human being is disqualified. We should hesitate before pushing to that conclusion because Paul would make an exception for Abraham (4:1–5) and maybe for others, including godly gentiles, but that is not said.

Instead he points to Jesus' death as providing the only means to rescue human beings and makes it the basis for his claim that through this event God now offers a right relationship (justification) and that this is a gift, not something to be earned or qualified for by keeping the law. He makes this explicit:

> But now, apart from the law, the righteousness of God has been disclosed, and is attested by the law and the prophets, 22the righteousness of God through faith in Jesus Christ for all who believe. For there is no distinction, 23since all have sinned and fall short of the glory of God; 24they are now justified by his grace as a gift, through the redemption that is in Christ Jesus, 25whom God put forward as a sacrifice of atonement by his blood, effective through faith. (3:21–25)

Paul on the Law

Paul then had to explain the status of the law. It was, after all, God's law. To do so, Paul draws on insights of his time as well as his own reflections. Thus, he suggests the law in effect made people face up to the fact they were all sinners (5:20). Indirectly it therefore consigned people into the hopeless situation of guilt. He also argued that this entrapment was also the result of the power of sin over generations, which like a disease made people sick. Adam's sin started the process (5:12–14).

Using the popular psychology of the day Paul also argued that the law, though in itself good and given by God, could be counterproductive (7:7–13). By forbidding certain acts it raised people's awareness that such sins were options, whereas they might never have occurred to them. As something good, itself, it produced something bad. Paul then gave an image of the human mind as divided within itself, wanting at one level to do good, but at another level wanting to do evil, knowing what is good as portrayed in God's law, but doing the opposite (7:14–25). This is an exposition of the state of humanity before the good news of Christ comes to the rescue.

He, therefore, affirms, that according to his gospel it is possible to be rescued from this captivity and the condemnation we deserve. He writes:

> For the law of the Spirit of life in Christ Jesus has set you free from the law of sin and of death. 3For God has done what the law, weakened by the flesh, could not do: by sending his own Son in the likeness of sinful flesh, and to deal with sin, he condemned sin in the flesh, 4so that the just requirement of the law might be fulfilled in us, who walk not according to the flesh but according to the Spirit. (8:2–4)

The law could not achieve this. Playfully he contrasts it with a new law, which is rather a new dynamic possibility. For, Paul argues, through sending Jesus, God offered to humanity a relationship of acceptance and love that can free people from guilt and from bondage. He goes further by adding that this new relationship in fact makes it possible for people to live lives that more than fulfill what the law commanded. In other words, Paul is arguing, this new relationship based on love generates loving behaviors that go far beyond what keeping the commandments might achieve.

Elsewhere he speaks of the Spirit of God generating fruit in the believer and these fruit include love, joy, peace, longsuffering, gentleness, goodness, faith, meekness, and temperance (Gal 5:22–23). To the Corinthians he had written that the true mark of the Spirit of God in people's lives is love, celebrated in his famous chapter on love (1 Cor 13).

Paul's Wisdom

One of Paul's major contributions to Christian faith is his insight, simply put, that love generates love, goodness generates goodness. Parents often recognize that the key to producing healthy children lies less in telling them what they should do and not do, than in giving them the security of being loved and that this will usually show itself in similarly loving and healthy behavior.

The example of parenting reminds us that in the reality of bringing up children both elements play a role: on the one hand, providing a loving environment that helps young people value themselves and so not feel the need to engage in behaviors that are responses to low self-esteem; and, on the other hand, setting limits and guidelines.

We find both elements playing a role in Paul's own approach. His foundational assumption is that if we walk in the Spirit, we will produce the fruit of the Spirit in our behavior. Nevertheless, Paul also finds it necessary to point to appropriate and inappropriate behaviors, especially in the final sections of his letters. These appropriate behaviors are primarily in the area of human relations and so certainly coincide with the basic values enshrined in the ethical commandments of the law, such as murder, theft, adultery, and truthfulness.

Paul's approach is not to say that once one has a restored relationship with God, then one should keep the commandments, but rather that one should grow in one's restored relation with God and recognize the implications of what that relationship can generate and mean. As well as spontaneously expressing love, people also need some guidance to recognize how that might express itself in particular actions. It nevertheless remains true for Paul that believers are not under the law; they are under grace (7:4–6). The law has ceased to be the cornerstone of their relationship with God, unlike, for instance in Matthew and Luke.

Wisdom in John

We find a similar spirituality expressed in the Gospel according to John. Eternal life is life in relation to God and it should express itself in showing the same love for one another as God has shown to us or Christ has shown to us. This is clearly expressed in Jesus' instructions to his disciples:

> I give you a new commandment, that you love one another. Just as
> I have loved you, you also should love one another. By this every-
> one will know that you are my disciples, if you have love for one
> another. (13:34–35)

An author from the same circles extrapolates this commandment in
the first letter of John, not only exhorting believers to love one another, but
also grounding this exhortation in the affirmation that God is love.

> Beloved, let us love one another, because love is from God; every-
> one who loves is born of God and knows God. 8Whoever does not
> love does not know God, for God is love. (4:7–8)

> God is love, and those who abide in love abide in God, and God
> abides in them. (4:16)

For the Gospel writer, the law, which was God's gift, has fulfilled its
purpose, which was to point to Christ and to foreshadow the new way of
relating to God that has come in Christ.

> From his fullness we have all received, grace in place of grace.
> The law indeed was given through Moses; grace and truth came
> through Jesus Christ.* (1:16–17)

God gave the law, but now in place of that gift of grace has come the
new gift of grace. The author is careful never to disparage the law, but to
depict it as having pointed to its own demise. Through its earthly temple
and associated festivals, it foreshadowed the new heavenly reality that has
come to earth and is to be available for people. What was at the level of the
material and flesh on earth is now superseded by what is at the level of the
spiritual. The writer of the letter to the Hebrews similarly sees the old as
foreshadowing the new and uses popular Platonic categories to depict the
old as the earthly image of the heavenly reality (9:9–12; 10:1).

For the author of the Fourth Gospel, believers do not live according
to the law, but according to Christ and his core commands of love. The
values thus implied do, indeed, reflect the ethical values found in the Ten
Commandments, but it portrays obedience as directed not towards the law,
but to Christ.

Mark on the Law

The Gospel according to Mark is in many respects close to Paul in its approach, but differs from Paul in portraying Jesus as declaring that people will receive eternal life if they keep the commandments in the way that Jesus expounds them (10:17–22). The focus is, however, only these moral commandments, not those related, for instance, to food or purity.

This is clearly evident when Mark reports the incident where Jesus' disciples face criticism from some Pharisees because they do not ritually wash their hands before eating (7:1–5). Mark gives his non-Jewish readers background information about Jewish rites of washing of both implements and of themselves in order to remain ritually clean.

He has Jesus criticize their giving attention to such things while giving too little to ethical issues (7:6–13), but then makes a broader statement that declares external things such as food cannot make a person unclean in God's eyes, but simply enter the stomach and exit into the toilet (7:15–23). "Listen to me, all of you, and understand: there is nothing outside a person that by going in can defile, but the things that come out are what defile" (7:14–15). "'Do you not see that whatever goes into a person from outside cannot defile, since it enters, not the heart but the stomach, and goes out into the sewer?' (Thus he declared all foods clean.)" (7:18–19). What makes people unclean is their thoughts and attitudes. Here the focus falls on moral attitudes.

> For it is from within, from the human heart, that evil intentions come: fornication, theft, murder, adultery, avarice, wickedness, deceit, licentiousness, envy, slander, pride, folly. All these evil things come from within, and they defile a person. (7:21–23)

Mark summarizes what he sees as the import of Jesus' words, namely, that he thereby declared all foods clean (7:19). This in effect dismissed large sections of the biblical law and does so on the basis they did not in fact make sense. Such things never could render a person unclean. Probably in the original conflict Jesus meant rather that what comes out of a person matters more than what enters, without dismissing the food laws, but Mark is re-interpreting this in the light of the later developments that led to the inclusion of gentiles. Mark is more radical than either Paul or John in making the claim that the commandments about food never made sense in the first place.

Mark has deliberately placed this episode between his accounts of the feeding of 5,000 Jews (6:32–44) and 4,000 non-Jews (8:1–9) to underline that one of the major barriers separating them was now declared to be invalid, namely food laws. To reinforce the message, Mark places an anecdote after this declaration, which depicts Jesus as initially reluctant but nevertheless going on to be willing to cross traditional boundaries by responding positively to a Syrophoenician woman who seeks help for her daughter (7:24–30).

To return to where we began, Matthew could hardly be expected to take up this anecdote from Mark unaltered. After all, he had portrayed Jesus as declaring that not a jot or stroke of the law was to be set aside. He, therefore, subtly rewrites it, omitting Mark's summary of its import, namely that Jesus was declaring all things clean, and, instead, turning it into simply a rejection of the requirement about washing hands, which he knew was not in the biblical law (Matt 15:1–20). He also changes the feeding of the 4,000 so that it is now a feeding of Jews and takes place in Jewish not gentile territory. This made it fit the historical reality, namely that the mission to gentiles, which Mark's story was foreshadowing symbolically, did not begin till after Easter (28:18–20).

Luke, too, could hardly be expected to agree, for, he, too, like Matthew insisted that not a stroke of the law should be set aside. His solution is radical. He omits this large section of Mark altogether, including the feeding of the 4,000, his largest omission of material from Mark. He does so in part also because he would deal with it in the book of Acts in his own way, as we have seen.

The Law Today

Do we still need the law? In the church today we will hear conflicting answers. But already in the New Testament we find conflicting answers, in part reflecting similar diversity within Judaism of the time. We need no more to tear ourselves apart over such differences than we need to tear apart the New Testament itself. There is one common stance and that is to reject the fundamentalist response that every commandment must stand. Matthew comes closest to having a fundamentalist stance, though no one really knows for sure whether, while not saying so, Matthew would have agreed to set circumcision aside. Possibly he did.

Within the diversity there is a further positive commonality: the focus on love, whether as the key to upholding the law or as the basis for an approach that leaves it aside. At best the interpretations of the law or of love identify a loving ongoing relationship as the best basis for developing loving behavior, which is guided by the law as providing God's guidelines for a loving life or grounded primarily in an appreciation and apprehension of God's love in Christ.

Relationship matters most and reality means we need at times informed advice about how that might best be lived out. That includes the way we best exercise that love in the world and become good news for the poor, but also how we relate to one another, including in conflict and grief. That was also going to be a challenge, as we shall see in the next chapter, and still is.

Reflection: What instances can you think of where informed love has needed to revise or even set aside what was once deemed to be law? Why was this so? What was the basis for such decisions?

8

Why Shame and Blame?

"I hate you! Why don't you love me?!"

Lecturer: My students are hopeless. They simply don't listen.
Lecturer's Spouse: Don't blame them. Have another look at the
substance and style of your lectures.

COPING WITH REJECTION IS never easy, especially when a person has emotional investment in not being rejected. The anger in "Why don't you love me?" above, arises from the desire to love and be loved, the more intense that desire, the stronger the anger and hate. Sometimes if you let anger have its space and listen to it, it will allow the feeling behind it to emerge, the fear or hurt or pain. Only then can we really deal with it and not bury it or let it build up till it explodes and causes havoc. Our anger is like our other feelings of hunger, sexual desire, pain, or even joy. They are part of how God made us. The issue is always what we do in responding to them.

People of the first generations of the faith were no different. This chapter explores some of the ways they dealt with their pain and their joy.

Rejection and Elation

In the first-century world of the expansion of the Jesus movement emotions ran high. At a very deep level they believed that what was at stake was life and death, and, as the movement developed, heaven and hell. This was something much more significant than slighted love. Genuine concern for people's fate mixed with deep hurt and disappointment when the good news, indeed, the love offered, met with a negative or indifferent response. That hurt could turn to anger and express itself in hateful outbursts.

It could also lead to attempts to explain to oneself and one's own why such responses were not positive, a kind of rationalizing of rejection and failure. People needed to be able to make sense of what had happened.

An opposite process could also take place when people sought to express their deep delight and appreciation that some responded positively, and that they themselves had done so. Sometimes this soared into exultant assertions that they had been chosen, indeed destined by God from before the foundation of the world, to be among the elect.

The writer of Ephesians begins his letter in such exultant jubilation:

> Blessed be the God and Father of our Lord Jesus Christ, who has blessed us in Christ with every spiritual blessing in the heavenly places, 4just as he chose us in Christ before the foundation of the world to be holy and blameless before him in love. 5He destined us for adoption as his children through Jesus Christ, according to the good pleasure of his will, 6to the praise of his glorious grace that he freely bestowed on us in the Beloved. (1:3–6)

Like the negative, this, too, has its equivalent in human relations where love soars into poetic claims that the loved partner was destined to be so before all time, the one "meant alone for me." We understand the elation, even if the reality is that one could probably have a successful marriage with perhaps even one in four people if one worked at it.

Words not only say things. They also do things, sometimes quite independently of what they say or at least at a level much more important than their literal meaning. "You were meant for me" is like that. We understand what these words are doing. They are not propounding a theory. They are not to be read as science.

A Closed System of Insiders and Outsiders?

The elation of insiders can, but need not, imply something negative about outsiders. Mostly we should be satisfied with appreciating what people are doing in such elation and sit lightly to it, but this has not always been the case. Sometimes the claims appear to set up distinctions that are absolute. This is a possible way of reading the following statement in the Gospel according to John:

> And this is the judgment, that the light has come into the world, and people loved darkness rather than light because their deeds were evil. For all who do evil hate the light and do not come to the light, so that their deeds may not be exposed. But those who do what is true come to the light, so that it may be clearly seen that their deeds have been done in God.' (3:19–21)

That appears to be a closed system. Those who do what is true come to the light. The others do not. End of story! We find similar statements in the sectarian documents found at Qumran in caves by the Dead Sea. There are children of light and children of darkness. Yet both in Qumran and in John there is a clear assumption that the distinctions are far from pre-determined or set. By responding to the message of the people of light, people of darkness can become children of light. Indeed, within the same chapter in John's Gospel, just three verses earlier we read:

> For God so loved the world that he gave his only Son, so that everyone who believes in him may not perish but may have eternal life. (3:16)

Some have tried to weave this possibility into a system of thought based on determinism with explanations, such as that God determined that these people would move from one group to the other, because they were chosen to do so before all time, just as those who refused the transition were predetermined not to do so. Pushed to the extreme such thinking leads to the conclusion, at worst, that God chooses to love and save some people, and to damn others, a huge problem for anyone wanting to argue that God is loving.

Instead, it is better to recognize that such statements, which seem to imply a closed system, have a function. What they are *doing* is more important than what they are *saying*. And what they are saying needs to be appreciated as an expression of gratitude and thanksgiving. They are in that sense performative utterances whose function is something other than making statements about reality, let alone doctrine. There is a tolerable inconsistency in insisting that some were never meant to respond while encouraging them to do so. Such is the way language can function.

Such statements can however fulfill important roles for those who make them when they are meant literally. They help them rationalize why some people reject their message. This goes beyond a healthy response, which accepts that some people will reject what we say. Claiming that there is something wrong with them (like the lecturer does about students' responses above) is a rather unhealthy way of dealing with the disappointment and grief of rejection.

Rejection and Blame

Such pain and grief can move beyond rationalizing the rejection as "meant to be," determined by God, to outright blame. Such is the explanation that the author of the Fourth Gospel dares to put on the lips of Jesus when he has Jesus declare that "the Jews," that is those Jews who do not respond positively to his message, are children of the devil (8:44). Bedeviling those who reject you is extreme. It is what one might expect to hear in a tantrum where rationality goes by the wayside. Placed in a composition designed to portray Jesus, it rightly wins little respect.

Why so angry? Why so bitter? The best explanation of the data here and elsewhere in the Fourth Gospel is that it is written in a context where people, many of them Jews themselves, are having to grapple with the fact that other Jews do not accept their message and what they claim about Jesus. The other Jews believe that the claim about Jesus goes too far. They see it as threatening the core of their faith, because it seems to imply that Jesus was not a human being and to make him into a second god. The author tries to show that this is a misunderstanding, but feelings ran high.

Dealing with rejection is never easy, especially if it is rejection by those to whom you want to be near or to whom you have been near in the past. Such would have been the experience of many in the emerging church of the first century in contrast to the somewhat offhand or coldly judgmental dismissal of rejection by later generations who had no sense of ever having belonged to Israel. Families were breaking up. Conflict was painful.

What in the context of the fourth gospel and its community were accusations, which belonged in that sense to a bitter family dispute between believing and unbelieving Jews, came in different contexts to be a source for more absolute claims about unbelieving Jews and Judaism. We soon had non-Jews taking such words out of their context and using them as a weapon of attack. Over the centuries this then developed to the extremes of Jew-hating, which became fairly widespread.

Anti-Semitism, which had pre-Christian roots, exploited such texts to declare Jews God-killers. Nazi propaganda combined it with conspiracy theories about their financial power to instigate hatred and the extermination of six million Jews in the Holocaust. The statements were reprehensible in the first place, but taken as more than performative utterances and as statements of reality, they were poison.

Jesus and Rejection

The reflections on rejection begin early. Jesus' own rejection by many of his fellow Jews and then by the Roman authorities was a core element of his story. He clearly did confront those who opposed him. But there is little evidence that he engaged in wholesale blaming or in declaring that people were never meant to respond and so were never loved by God. The conflicts with some of the Pharisees were over the substance and interpretation of the law, but one does not get the impression that Jesus permanently wrote them off.

His parables address rejection. Famously the parable of the sower, which asserts that God's kingdom would have a harvest despite setbacks along the way, became a source for reflecting on success and failure (Mark 4:3–8). The explanations of why some seed successfully bore fruit, some never sprouted and some sprouted but then shriveled (4:13–20), were probably the product of secondary reflection within the movement. It may have simply been a way of their facing reality. It could easily become more than that, namely an explanation for their own failures combined with being a mechanism for coping with that grief by blaming the soils.

Mark even suggests that Jesus told parables in order to obscure the truth from all except those with the ability to see (4:10–12), a very counter-intuitive explanation, which is then somewhat undone by Mark depicting the disciples, the insiders supposed to be able to see, as themselves blind (8:14–21). Mark is thereby engaging not in history, but in the rhetoric of challenging his own hearers not to miss the meaning of Jesus' message. Matthew revises this to depict the disciples as lacking not in understanding but in faith (13:33–35). Neither, however, resorts to explanations that write them off as predetermined so to act.

Discrediting Dissent

Another strategy for self-assurance is to convince oneself that where those who reject you make claims to offer what you also offer, you demonstrate to them and yourself that those claims are false. This is surely a legitimate process if one sees false claims. Sometimes it is indeed an act of care and compassion to help people see that their assumptions and beliefs may be without foundation and even be harmful to them.

In experiences where what people offer is rejected the process can often go too far, so that instead of promoting what I know to be good and helpful, I also go on the offensive and attack or disparage the offerings of others, even to the extent of engaging in distortion and misrepresentation. There were developments within the Jesus movement that tended in this direction as there have been such developments ever since.

For centuries some Christians, especially Protestant Christians, caricatured Judaism as a religion of works. Stereotypically the analysis of what was wrong with Judaism was that it taught that we could claim acceptance and forgiveness from God only on the basis of earning it by doing good works, justification by works, an arrogant strategy. Of course, it was possible to find texts that appeared to embody such an attitude. We now, however, recognize the falsity of the claim.

It was also embarrassing for those making such a case that we also find the notion of judgment according to works in the New Testament (Matt 16:27). Indeed, Protestants have often put so much emphasis on believers working hard, the Protestant work ethic, that they have seemed to fall into the very same attitudes that they were so anxious to avoid.

The same stereotypical contrast found its way into the disputes between Protestant and Catholics. Thus, some Protestants accused Catholics of also teaching justification by works. There were some practices, such as paying for indulgences, that guaranteed forgiveness, which fit the stereotype. We have long since learned and acknowledged, however, that these are abuses and not fair or balanced representations of Catholic faith. Something goes badly wrong when conflict leads people to misrepresent their opponents.

Disqualifying Dissent

In the first century, as we have noted in an earlier chapter, there developed the notion that through his death on the cross Christ made it possible for people to be restored to a right relationship with God. At best it affirmed that in his death we see the same generous love that Jesus affirmed about God to his fellow Jews during his ministry.

When however in the context of conflict this became a claim that only through the death of Jesus such forgiveness and reconciliation is possible, underlined by depicting this as the required act to achieve atonement, this led, as noted in chapter 2 above, to the corollary that there was no other way and all other ways to claim forgiveness were false. Dealing with rejection of the gospel by fellow Jews now entailed also the claim that they and their faith had nothing to offer. At best such disqualification was meant to lead them to embrace the new Jewish movement of the followers of Jesus and leave their own faith behind.

This exclusivity, genuinely believed and strongly self-assuring for the believers, not only disqualified the faith of non-believing Jews, but also, by implication, largely unrecognized, the faith of Jesus himself and John the Baptist, both of whom affirmed, as good Jews, the faith that God forgives and restores. At best such a cross-centered Christianity reduces Jesus and his ministry to preliminaries, which included teaching useful for the guidance of those saved through the cross, but otherwise his proclamations were seen as simply wise teachings incidentally given while steering towards the main event.

Disqualifying one's former faith led some to a radical break, even to a bedeviling of Israel's God as a nasty heavenly being who created a nasty creation from which the higher and true God can rescue us through his divine Word appearing on earth in the person of Jesus. The church wisely rejected such constructions. The more common approach was to seek to hold continuity and discontinuity together.

Discontinuity and Continuity

The letter to the Hebrews does this, as we have seen in the previous chapter, by depicting what it calls the old covenant, based on the biblical law, as an earthly reflection of a higher heavenly reality, which has now come as the basis of a new covenant in Christ. The old is devalued, sometimes depicted as useless with regard to forgiveness of sins—how can the blood of bulls and goats achieve that!?—but nevertheless depicted as a God-inspired earthly copy, using Platonic categories (7:18; 10:1–4).

The old could never effect salvation and forgiveness, but it served only to foreshadow what can do so, namely the atonement wrought by Christ (9:11–14). This was a highly imaginative use of typology trimmed to fit the author's purpose to portray Jesus as high priest, atoning for all through his death. When the author refers to the greats of the Old Testament as "[our] fathers" (1:1), this probably indicates that he is writing as a converted Jew seeking to explain how and why the old came to be replaced by the new. The old covenant was foreshadowing and predicting. Thus, he could claim continuity, but there was also discontinuity, because the new covenant has come and, by implication, not to embrace it but to remain with the old, was to reject God. This reductionist portrait of Israel's faith hardly does it justice.

The same logic informs the exclusivity in John. God gave the law through Moses (1:17), but, as noted in the previous chapter, at an earthly level it pointed forward and foreshadowed what was to come. Thus, as in Hebrews, people who remain with the old and resist the new are resisting God and demonized as God's enemies and children of the devil.

At the same time the author of the Fourth Gospel has not treated Jesus' death as so exclusive that it reduces Jesus' ministry to a prelude, but embraces the notion that what the law was once believed to offer as God's Wisdom, namely the bread of life, the living water, the light and truth, is now offered in reality in the person of Jesus who alone is God's Wisdom and Word. His approach is exclusive but not in a way that implicitly disqualifies Jesus himself, though unlike the other Gospels he does, as we have seen in chapter 3, ensure that John the Baptist is no longer seen as a medium of forgiveness, reducing his role to a witness who points to the true source of eternal life, Jesus.

Luke deals with the issues of continuity and discontinuity partly by depicting the story of Jesus and the church as matching stories of old, such as in the forty days of the risen Jesus' appearances matching the forty years in the wilderness and the symbolic use of twelve, not only for the twelve apostles whose number is reconstituted after Judas' failure, but also for the 120 (12 x 10) in the upper room (Acts 1:15).

In addition, however, he has the story of Jesus introduced by legends surrounding the birth of John and Jesus, which depict faithful devout Jews. Similarly, in introducing the story of the church he has faithful devout Jews, now believers in Jesus, worshiping in the temple. The implicit claim is that the Jesus movement, far from being an offshoot of Israel, let alone a sect, is in fact true Israel and those Jews who do not make the transition must be seen as guilty of not following God's will and plan (Acts 28:24–28).

As noted in the previous chapter, neither Luke nor Matthew advocates setting the law aside or substantial parts of it as does Mark, who appears to retain only the moral commandments. Matthew's account of Jesus has particularly sharp criticisms of Pharisees and scribes, who in Matthew's day dominate the synagogues and clearly refuse to accept the claims of Matthew and his community about Jesus as the Messiah (Matthew 23). Matthew's disqualification of them does not descend to bedevilment, but focuses on moral depravity and hypocrisy, namely failing to uphold the law. It nevertheless has a similar level of bitterness as that found in John's Gospel consistent with the emotions typical of a family feud and as noted above reaches sad depths in depicting Jerusalem's sacking and the slaughter of so many of its citizens as their own fault for rejecting the Christian message (22:1–14; 27:25).

Paul on Continuity and Discontinuity

Paul's ministry was beset with opposition both from unbelieving Jews and from believing Jews and others who saw him compromising what according to Scripture and their view God demanded. Far from employing hateful or dismissive rhetoric towards unbelieving Israel, Paul shows himself deeply pained by Israel's rejection of the gospel (Rom 9:1–2), and even then cannot bring himself to dismiss them or their faith as no longer loved by God.

While in Galatians he emphasized discontinuity (4:21–31), it is revealing of his deep sense of connection that by the time he writes Romans he resolves the matter of their opposition not by argument or accusation, but by engaging in the language of mystery. God cannot give up on them, but how he will win them over must be left as a mystery (Rom 11:25–31). "I want you to understand this mystery: a hardening has come upon part of Israel, until the full number of the Gentiles has come in. 26And so all Israel will be saved" (11:25–26). Love generates hope that remains in the dark. He was, however, far more strident in rejecting fellow believers who attacked him and had sought to persuade his churches in Galatia that they should submit to circumcision, declaring them accursed by God (Gal 1:6–9) and in a moment of anger writing that they should go and castrate themselves (5:12).

One of the other means for bolstering assurance and also dealing with the continuity and discontinuity issue was by claiming fulfillment of Scripture. We return to this in detail in chapter 9. This was especially important for Jews who became believers, but also for others, for part of their faith, too, entailed belief that the Jewish Scripture had an authoritative role. To be able to show that this or that event or saying was predicted or prefigured in Scripture gave that event or saying extra warrant. We saw in an earlier chapter how it helped shape the account of Jesus' death and so to make sense of it. In the next chapter we shall explore how this process worked and shaped also other materials in the Gospels.

On Not Denigrating Dissent

At one level the confidence that we are loved and accepted by God can remove from us the need to bolster our identity by denying what others claim, let alone deeming them hopeless or even evil. You do not need to denigrate those who do not agree with you, even if you are sure they are wrong. Love and respect can acknowledge the right of others to their viewpoint. Conflict of ideas does not need to become conflict of persons, as happens so frequently.

Affirming our own understandings does not imply going along also with every other view in order to keep the peace. Every positive affirmation stands in opposition to what it contradicts. To affirm men and women as God's good creation implies rejecting the notion of inequality, let alone abuse. If our beliefs have substance and matter, they will inevitably be in conflict with other viewpoints. If our beliefs matter, we will want to argue for them. Affirming love will bring us into conflict with those who do not, whether as individuals, as religious people, or as politicians.

The problem is when we move from disagreement, even vehement disagreement, to vilification. We can see this happening sometimes when people sense their arguments are not persuasive and resort to shouting or thumping the lectern. Flipping over from civil and respectful disagreement to acts of vilification where we call the other's integrity into question and, using religious discourse, to declare them enemies of God, is violence and abuse of the integrity of the other and not love.

One of the helpful developments in recent years within the world of Christian reflection has been the realization that from its beginnings Christian people have found ways of turning away from the principle of love and respect for the other and have engaged in abusive behavior. Abusive behavior is never justified and never necessary and runs contrary to the teaching of Jesus and to love and respect, wherever its light may shine, in whatever religion or culture. For, as Jesus showed in his parables, there is a common understanding of what love means where people are engaged in human relations, especially in being family. God is at least as good as a good and caring parent and people know what that means.

There is never any justification for making up falsehoods about people with whom we are in conflict, nor for telling lies about ourselves. When we embrace love, from God, for God, for ourselves and for others, we can face up to ourselves as we are and accept others as they are even when we disagree. Truth is a casualty of fear and as the writer of 1 John in another context put it:

> There is no fear in love; for perfect love casts out fear. (4:18)

Reflection: How can one disagree without denigrating? What are implications for interfaith dialogue?

9

"Telling Lies for God"?

"It was enormous. Must have been at least 3 feet long! Wait till I tell my friends at school."

Next Day: "Yesterday I caught this fish—4 feet long and just as I was pulling it in it slipped off the hook. Never seen anything like it!"

THE FISH THAT GOT away is just one example of many, reflecting a human tendency to exaggerate. You would hardly call it lying, but, of course, it is also not true. Gospel writers were just like the rest of us in their enthusiasm. Where Mark, for instance, speaks of a crowd and tells us that Jesus healed *many* people (1:32–34), Matthew and Luke make the claim he healed *all* (Matt 8:16; Luke 4:40–41)! Where Mark tells us that Simon's mother-in-law had a fever (1:29–31), in Luke we read that it was a *great* fever (Luke 4:38–39). These are samples from Mark's opening chapter. Matthew and Luke did not have independent sources in these instances. They simply enhanced the stories for effect. There are many more such instances. The enthusiasm that generates such exaggeration reflects a desire to impress, our school mates about the size of the fish, or followers of Jesus about how wonderful Jesus was.

Tall Stories?

In the world of the first century, teachers often sought to enhance their credentials by claiming to be able to do extraordinary things. Their followers were even more likely to promote their teachers in this way. Emperors, too, sought to enhance their authority in this way, including with claims to miraculous powers. In an age of greater credulity there was an open market for claims and counterclaims, a competition for authority and status.

This was certainly a feature in the Jesus movement and the claims about Jesus became more fantastic as time passed. This cannot simply be put down to invention. There were reports that Jesus did some things that people of his day saw as miraculous and their existence encouraged the trend. It is hard to make sense of what appear to be authentic claims that what he was doing indicated that the reign of God was breaking in his ministry if he had not done anything to warrant the claim.

Embarrassing as it will be for people in the modern world, the evidence suggests that he did practice exorcism and that he did perform acts of healing, including using the methods and means of his day such as spittle and touch and addressing evil spirits. Unless we embrace the presuppositions that he and his contemporaries had about demons and causation, many of these stories strain our credibility and our natural inclination will be to assess them in the same way we would assess such claims today.

Integrity and truth are important, including for people with faith. We should seek to be consistent in our approach to reality because they were not living in a fantasy "Bible land," but in the same world as us, which operated under the same conditions. For some, such stories then and now are credible and accounted for by the intervention of divine powers, indeed the Spirit of God. For others, like myself, such stories call for explanation on the assumptions that I bring to every other part of daily life. This means, indeed, that not all will find my reflections in this chapter convincing.

Miracles to Match the Prophets of Old

There can be little doubt that we have a string of miracle stories told about Jesus that reflect and indeed have been shaped at least in their telling, if not in their substance, by stories told about prophets like Moses, Elijah, and Elisha. Some would limit that influence to the way the story is told and see it as a way of evoking those stories and so seeing Jesus as in some way in continuity with them. I find it more persuasive to see these as stories that have in part or in full been generated by such stories with that aim.

Such stories are the raising from the dead of a widow's son (Luke 7:11–17), just as Elijah and Elisha did (1 Kgs 17:17–24; 2 Kgs 4:32–37), the miraculous feeding of a crowd with few resources, as Elijah and Elisha did (1 Kgs 17:8–16; 2 Kgs 4:38–44), as well as miracles with the sea, which recall Moses' exploits. Walking on water and stilling storms reflect imagery from the Psalms of the acts of Yahweh (107:24–29; 77:19), the latter shaped also by the story of Jonah (1:4–18).

It would be an enormous benefit if people of the Jesus movement could also have such powers and the church then be a repository of abilities to perform sea rescues by stilling storms and walking over oceans, and not least, if it retained the magical ability to feed hungry people. It is tragic if not downright offensive to have such claims made in contexts where people are dying of hunger.

Symbolic Stories?

The resolution to such dilemmas has been to declare that these were one-off wonders, non-repeatable, and were designed primarily to impress, not to set a pattern of how Jesus and his followers might help people. I find it more plausible to acknowledge that these are narratives largely generated by the powerful symbolism that they embody.

The waters of the deep represented something fearful for many Jews in landlocked Israel. This is not difficult to understand. It was the place of evil spirits, symbolized in the pigs who in the story Jesus sends to their death in the lake (Mark 5:1–20). To depict Jesus as able to walk over the deep (Mark 6:45–52) was a way of declaring that he could address and overcome such fears and dangers, in particular, the deep fears people held about death. The story is a statement about authority and the claim to bring the love and forgiveness that sets people free. Matthew embellishes the story by having Peter also invited to walk on water, the symbolic "rock" (his name's meaning) on which the church would be built (Matt 14:22–33).

Stilling the storm, narrated as an exorcism, where Jesus rebukes the spirits of the wind that produced it, has been a favorite image for describing the peace that the gospel of Jesus brings and the need to trust in the face of adversity.

The feedings of the 5,000 and the 4,000 are full of symbolism, including numeric symbolism. Mark's account of the feeding of the 5,000 (6:32–44) describes the people as like sheep without a shepherd, a favorite Old Testament image of Israel (e.g. Num 27:17; 2 Chr 18:16). The figure of 5,000 is probably meant to evoke the fact that there are five books in the law (Genesis to Deuteronomy), perhaps also the five loaves and two fish function similarly. The number of twelve baskets of leftovers reflects the tradition of the twelve tribes of Israel. This feeding takes place in Jewish territory and symbolizes the gospel coming to Israel. Food was a common metaphor for good news; both brought hope and nourishment.

Mark then locates the feeding of the 4,000 in gentile territory (8:1–9). In the ancient world four symbolizes the four corners of the earth, the four directions. There are seven baskets of leftovers, seven symbolizing the universal and perhaps represented in the starting resources being seven loaves.

Mark's use of symbolism extends across chapters 6–8, where in chapter 7, between the two feedings, we have the controversy about eating food with unwashed hands, which we discussed in chapter 7. Here, Mark has Jesus declare that no food can make people unclean, thus declaring biblical laws that were instrumental in keeping Jews and gentiles apart as not only no longer applicable but also as never having made sense (7:1–23). To reinforce the insight, he brings the story of Jesus helping a Syrophoenician woman, despite his expressing the reluctance traditional for some Jews in his setting (7:24–30).

Indeed, we find that Mark not only has Jesus confront the disciples for not seeing the symbolism in the numbers twelve and seven (8:15–21), but also goes on to depict their blindness to his message of what true greatness means. He does this by surrounding the section that reaches from mid chapter 8 to the end of chapter 10 with two stories about blind men being made to see (8:22–26; 10:45–52), symbolically contrasting them with the disciples' inner blindness. Here we have literary creativity at work in the symbolic treatment of miracle stories.

Matthew also uses the story of the healing of the blind man that Mark had placed at the end of chapter 10, in a similar way, but in even more daring fashion. He drops the name of the blind man, Bartimaeus, and instead makes it a story about two blind men. In Jewish law two witnesses carried authoritative weight. He goes even further by using the story twice, in chapter 9, in a collection of Jesus' deeds (9:27–31) and in its original place as found in Mark, just before Jesus' entry into Jerusalem (20:29–34).

Miracle stories are clearly serving a purpose other than crude propaganda and can be embellished to achieve the aim. Telling lies for God? That would be harsh, but certainly going far beyond anything which could be claimed to be history. Nor was this deceit, because people would have known about such playfulness and symbolism in storytelling and proclamation, even though mostly they would still see a core of history in such stories, though subordinate in significance.

Countering Miracle-Based Faith in John's Gospel

It is very likely that the author of the Fourth Gospel had recourse to a collection or collections of miracles, which appear to have been told at some stage primarily for the impact of the miraculous. The account of the healing of the official's boy at a distance (4:46–54) gives at least half of the length of the story to emphasizing that it was exactly at the time that Jesus promised the healing that it occurred. That was a "wow" factor and typical of miracles told for propaganda purposes.

Some of the other miracle stories in John's collection are similar and are typical of the trend towards the sensational, which came about as the movement developed. Turning water into wine (2:1–11) was a magical event that put Jesus right up there with others who allegedly performed such feats. Raising Lazarus from the dead (11:1–44) was all the more spectacular because he had been dead for four days. People believed that the soul hovered by the body for only three days.

There is little doubt that some within the Jesus movement sought to win followers for Jesus on the basis of the mighty miracles they claimed he performed. Sometimes these miracles were told as acts of compassion, but mostly that was not the case. There was usually little interest in what happened to those who were healed. The focus was solely on the greatness of Jesus, the hero. It was one thing to win followers. It was another to ask: follow him for what? If miracles proved his authority, indeed his divinity, what was the message? Was it just adulation?

The Gospel according to John is very interesting in this respect because the author depicts Jesus as not at all happy with people who followed him just because of his miracles. Very early in his Gospel he reports Jesus' hesitation about such following.

> When he was in Jerusalem during the Passover festival, many
> believed in his name because they saw the miracles that he was

doing. 24But Jesus on his part would not believe in them, because he knew all people 25and needed no one to testify about man; for he himself knew what was in man.* (2:23–25)

This non-inclusive rendering, which simply reproduces the Greek as "man," helps us recognize the strong connection to what follows, for the author goes on to write: "Now there a *man* from the Pharisees, Nicodemus" (3:1). Thus, Nicodemus serves as an example of people who "believed in his name," a common technical expression for becoming a believer, on the basis of the miracles. The author has him declare:

Rabbi, we know that you have come from God, because no one can do these miracles which you are doing, unless God is with him. (3:2)

Dissatisfied with that kind of faith, Jesus challenges Nicodemus:

Truly, truly I tell you, unless a person is born from above he cannot see the kingdom of God. (3:3)

Traditionally used in Christianity as a text to address non-believers, this text is addressed to a believer who approaches Jesus with the wrong kind of faith. The author at no point calls the miracles into question, but he insists that to have faith in Jesus means to understand that he came to make God known, to offer God's eternal life. He did not come to seek adulation from people who are impressed with miracles. There is so much more to faith than that.

We find a similar rebuke embodied in the story of the official's son, cited above, where the author has Jesus address everyone in the plural with the rebuke: "Unless you see signs and wonders you will not believe!" (4:48). Similarly, the author describes the response of the crowds after the feeding of the 5,000:

When the people saw the sign that he had done, they began to say, "This is indeed the prophet who is to come into the world." When Jesus realized that they were about to come and take him by force to make him king, he withdrew again to the mountain by himself. (6:14–15)

That is not the kind of response or faith Jesus was looking for according to the author. In what is a remarkable achievement, the author of the Fourth Gospel takes the old stories, including the miracles stories, and weaves them into a narrative, which he enriches with fictional dialogues that portray Jesus as explaining himself and his significance in language and concepts that had clearly become central in his community.

His use of the feeding of the 5,000 is a prime example. He uses it to have Jesus declare that he is the bread of life (6:26–51). Partly this is to counter the claim of fellow Jews that the law was like the manna from heaven, which people needed (6:32). Partly it was a way of declaring Jesus' significance. He and he alone is the source of eternal life, the true bread. The author can also supplement this with reference to the time after Easter by speaking of Jesus' flesh and blood, represented in the Eucharist, as being the source of divine food (6:51–58).

Underlying such claims is not an image of Jesus as separate from God, but rather of Jesus as the conduit or pointer to God. God is the source of eternal life and the author's claim is that Jesus mediates this life because of what he says and does, and above all because of who he is, as God's own Word embodied in real human flesh and blood (1:14).

This enables the author to use miracle stories to express this truth in symbolism. Thus, as he had done with the feeding of the 5,000 in having Jesus claim, "I am the true bread," so he makes Jesus' healing a blind man the basis for the claim: "I am the light of the world" (9:5; also 8:12) and Lazarus' resurrection, the basis for the claim: "I am the resurrection and the life" (11:25). Indeed, the focus of the latter is so much on the symbolism that this claim somewhat jars with the literal story that assumes Lazarus would, indeed, die at some time. Some even see in the use of the words "I am" a claim to speak for God as the great "I am".

Correcting Miracle-Based Faith Elsewhere

Correction of miracle-based faith occurs in other places in the New Testament, largely with the exception of Luke who comes closest to using miracles for propaganda purposes. For he appears to want to paint the time of Jesus and first generation of the apostles as a kind of golden age of special divine intervention.

The problem with such miracle-based faith is that it encouraged the notion that if you followed Jesus, you would have access to powers that would guarantee you success. The major difficulty with that perspective is that it cannot account for the fact that on that scale of values Jesus was not successful or had a different set of priorities because his ministry ended with suffering and execution. This lay behind the reaction against miracle-based faith rather than the modern skepticism we might bring to such accounts.

Matthew addresses this in a striking way when he has Jesus declare at the conclusion of the Sermon on the Mount:

> Not everyone who says to me, "Lord, Lord", will enter the kingdom of heaven, but only one who does the will of my Father in heaven. 22On that day many will say to me, "Lord, Lord, did we not prophesy in your name, and cast out demons in your name, and do many deeds of power in your name?" 23Then I will declare to them, "I never knew you; go away from me, you evildoers." (7:21–23)

In this way Matthew is having Jesus address people of his own time who, he claims, miss the point of what it means to have faith in and follow Jesus. A quarter of a century earlier Paul had to confront such faith in the communities he founded in Corinth where the mark of the Spirit was taken to be miracles. Paul does not deny miracles, but, as noted in an earlier chapter, makes it very clear that the sign of the Spirit's life in the believer is love (1 Cor 13).

Earlier he had confronted models of power and wisdom claimed by some by declaring that he preached the cross, calling it a sign of the weakness and foolishness of God, seen from the perspective of human beings' notions of the power and wisdom that they value (1 Cor 1:18–25). Paul saw greatness, including the greatness of God and Christ, as expressed in lowliness and love. Mark would, as we have seen, take up this theme.

The drive therefore to embellish and enhance the miraculous in order to win admirers for Jesus thus met a corrective. That corrective did not, however, address the fictional elaborations that were developed for propaganda nor the fact that while not telling lies such stories certainly went beyond the truth to the point where not only false claims but also a false spirituality was the result.

Fulfilling Scripture

Another element that fed early Christian activity was, as noted in relation to miracles stories and to the narratives of Jesus' crucifixion, the attempt to depict Jesus as in some way reflecting patterns of divine power already portrayed in the great prophets. More directly, such impact flowed also from attempts to provide warrant and authorization for Jesus and his message on the basis that he fulfilled Old Testament prophecies.

To see one's own time as the time to which prophets pointed was a means of not only claiming authority but also of engendering hope, especially when those prophecies promised a successful outcome. The Jewish sect whose writings are preserved among the documents found in the caves at Qumran on the shores of the Dead Sea read the Old Testament prophets as referring to the conflicts in which they had been engaged. Scripture was in that sense read as a timeless inspired authority, so the meaning of statements in their original context was rarely in view.

When Christians did the same, it was not as though they were being deliberately deceitful. They were taking biblical statements as references to themselves, just as the people of that sect did. Matthew introduces a number of quotations with the words, "This was to fulfill what was spoken by the prophet, saying . . . " and variants of the same. Accordingly, using the Greek version, he cites Isaiah 7:14, which originally predicted impending relief from the threat of the Assyrian army, to refer to Jesus' birth and his mother as a "virgin." The Hebrew read "young woman" and simply means that relief will come in in as short a time as it takes for a young woman to conceive and give birth to a child. For Matthew it is a prophecy of Jesus' birth to Mary as a virgin.

Nearly all such "prophecies" are taken out of context and applied imaginatively to add warrant and authority to the stories being told. That worked for people then. It can scarcely work for us today with our commitment to hearing what people say in their context and their terms, but we can understand why they did so, based on their genuine beliefs that Scripture transcended context and carried meaning independent of its origins.

Fiction and Faith

Fiction, however, developed not only in order to promote faith, but also to defend it. Sadly, this led to denigration of Jews and Jewish leaders that left truth behind, as we saw in the previous chapter. Such is Matthew's insertion into the story of Jesus' death, that the Jerusalem crowds declared that Jesus' blood be upon them and on their children (27:25). Matthew, indeed, interpreted the terrible slaughter and destruction that accompanied the suppression of the rebellion of the first Jewish war in the successful siege of

Jerusalem by the Roman armies as God's vengeance on the people for Jesus' death and the rejection of the Christian mission (22:1–14).

The fictional elaborations in the account in John's Gospel of Jesus' trial before Pilate also cruelly portray the Jewish leaders as betraying their own faith and being chiefly to blame for Jesus' death with Pilate only weak, as in Matthew, and thereby Rome all but exonerated for what was a Roman execution.

The conflicts between believers in the Jesus movement and their fellow Jews led to a shaping of the anecdotes telling of Jesus' conflicts in a way that shunted home to them the guilt for Jesus' death. Much of this is misrepresentation, falsehoods told to sure up the movement. Indeed, one must acknowledge, it was engaging in falsehood, and in that sense, "telling lies for God," at least for their image of God.

I first met the title of this chapter as the name of a book by a geologist, Ian Plimer, *Telling Lies for God* (Sydney: Random House Australia, 1994), who used it to confront creationists who misrepresented data about the complexities of evolution in order to discredit the theory. It is, sadly, a common place where blind faith turns its back on open dialogue and informed discussion.

The early Christian movement was in that sense rather a mixed bag in relation to its ethical values. At its best it bore a message of love, true to the one who inspired it. At its worst it created grounds for division and abuse, untrue to what were allegedly its core values. It is nevertheless explicable in the light of the values and trends of its context, which also in a broader sense were both good news and bad news for human community.

For reflection: In what ways do you see miracle-based faith and notions of faith leading to success and prosperity alive in Christianity today?

10

Does the Bible Tell It All
on Sex and Marriage?

I tell you, whoever looks at a woman and finds her sexually attractive has already committed adultery with her in his mind. (with apologies to Matt 5:28)

IT IS, INDEED, POSSIBLE to translate this saying attributed to Jesus in the Sermon on the Mount along these lines and people have done so. The implications include that the sexual feelings people have in response to others are themselves sinful—as bad as adultery itself, and that since this is a statement addressing men, they should see women and their sexuality as an ever-present danger.

For those who read the Old Testament in the Greek translation this might be reinforced in the story of the temptation of Eve in the garden of Eden, where it translates the Hebrew word in Gen 3:13 which meant tricked or deceived by a Greek word which, unlike the Hebrew, also meant seduced. It was possible then to see the sin that set sin off running in the world as a sexual sin, the snake's seduction of Eve, and indeed some did, such as Paul (2 Cor 11:3).

The statement attributed to Jesus in Matt 5:28, when read as implying that sexual feeling is sinful, as it was often understood, had major repercussions. It made men (and women) feel guilty about their sexuality and made men anxious about women, leading them often to impose restrictions on women, insisting that they be covered up and controlled, and certainly kept away from positions of leadership where they might wittingly or unwittingly seduce men.

A More Careful Reading

Was that really what Matthew originally intended Jesus' saying to mean? In part to answer that question we must start by reading it in its original language, Greek, and then we must read it in its cultural context, so that we can know what Matthew and those listening to Matthew would have understood in their day. Taking the Bible seriously, indeed taking anyone seriously means trying to listen to what they are saying in their context and certainly not hearing only what we want to hear or reading into what was said what we would prefer to hear.

On the level of language there is a phrase in the Greek that could mean either "for the purpose that" or "with the result that." Was the saying talking about looking at a woman for the purpose of wanting to have intercourse with her or about looking at a woman with the result that one might find her attractive and so want to have sexual intercourse with her? Both options are possible if we consider only the words in isolation. If, however, we look at how Matthew used that phrase elsewhere in his Gospel, it is clear that he means the former, namely looking at a woman for the purpose of wanting to have sexual intercourse with her. He is not writing about people having feelings of sexual attraction towards someone. He is writing about what people do with those feelings, looking with a view to wanting to commit adultery.

Sexual Feelings Sinful?

This is confirmed when we consider the context in which Matthew was writing. That context means both Matthew's religious and his social context. To begin with, does the religious tradition that Jesus represents and that Matthew and his community strongly affirm indicate sexual feelings are, themselves, sinful? Here the answer is unambiguous. Sexual feelings are not in themselves right or wrong, any more than feelings of hunger and the desire for food are. They are part of how God created people to be. Creation is fundamental to Jewish faith, including that of Matthew and Jesus himself. Feelings become wrong when wrongly directed. This is obvious with the feeling of hunger. Uncontrolled it ends in the self-abuse of obesity.

In the case of sexual feelings, it could lead to abuse of others. But in both cases it might also lead to what is good and wholesome.

When in the story of Adam and Eve we are told that they covered their private parts with fig leaves (Gen 3:7), this was not because they saw their genitalia as sinful. It was rather reflecting the modesty characteristic of most societies told as a legendary story to explain its origins. Modesty in a world where sin had made its way was in part about defending oneself against potential abuse.

The story of the creation of man and woman in Genesis 1—2 affirms humanity as God's creation and as good. This includes the feelings that belong to the body. In particular, the creation myth relates the desire of the male and the female to re-join as the result of how they were created, the woman being extracted from the man (Gen 2:20-24). The assumption is that the desire to join, to engage in sexual intercourse, is part of what is God-given in creation.

> Therefore a man leaves his father and his mother and clings to his wife, and they become one flesh. (Gen 2:24)

Jewish authors frequently appeal to the creation story in particular, to talk about marriage. Jesus as a Jew does the same (Mark 10:2–9). The Genesis story underlines the positive dimension of marriage as companionship, including sexual union in this way, when it has God declare:

> It is not good that the man should be alone; I will make him a helper as his partner. (2:18)

This all makes it very unlikely that Matthew intended Jesus' saying in the Sermon on the Mount to mean that sexual feelings, themselves, are evil and that women are accordingly to be seen as dangerous. The preferred translation consistent with Jesus' attitude and that of his fellow Jews was that looking at someone else's wife with a view to wanting to have her sexually is at least adultery in attitude and so to be seen as also an act of sin.

In effect Jesus was taking up what is already included in the last of the Ten Commandments:

> You shall not covet your neighbor's house; you shall not covet your neighbor's wife, or male or female slave, or ox, or donkey, or anything that belongs to your neighbor. (Exod 20:17)

The command in the first creation story to be fruitful and multiply (1:28), as the animals also had to do, had its own inner ally in human sexual desire. And the affirmation of companionship, including the intimacy of joining in the second creation story in Genesis 2, combined with this to enable people to see their sexuality as something healthy and positive. Sex is not just for creating offspring. It is also an expression of joined intimacy and companionship. Both elements belong and are good.

Why Adultery Mattered

The warning about adulterous attitudes and not just adulterous acts makes good sense in their culture as in ours. People knew about adultery. They certainly knew about sexuality. It was not a theoretical or obscure theme for abstract debate. Sexuality was right there, intimately present in their genitalia and, more importantly, in their brains, as much as it is also for us. It was not a matter about which they needed to be told. It was a matter that needed to be valued and controlled.

People both in Jewish culture and in Greek and Roman culture took adultery very seriously. They will have shared the experience of pain and hurt that adultery can generate. The Old Testament prophets, particularly Hosea, play on this in depicting God's hurt and anger when Israel went off after other gods as spiritual adultery.

In those cultures, however, there was much more at stake. As still in some cultures today, family was much more than mum and dad plus the children. People were much more connected together as extended families with multiple generations and also aunts, uncles, cousins, and the like. The extended family was also the major source of stability. Frequently it was where work was done, whether through home crafts or through agriculture.

It was the primary source for welfare and care of the sick and aged, sometimes tied to patrons and landlords who could provide such support. The future of the family enterprise was crucial. There needed to be members to work, to support those older members who might survive, and the wife needed to bear children to secure stable leadership for the future. Wives, apart from bearing children, were often the managers of the household, whereas the men managed affairs beyond the household, such as relations with patrons and other men.

Adultery, therefore, not only threatened to bring hurt and pain to a spouse. It threatened the stability of the whole extended family enterprise and could have serious consequences for all its members, all the more so when a male child born through adultery might bring foreign leadership into the mix. Adultery also amounted to theft, as the tenth commandment implied (Exod 20:17; Deut 5:21).

The seriousness with which all three cultures, Greek, Roman, and Jewish, viewed adultery is reflected in the laws that prohibited it and punished it. In Jewish law it warranted execution of both parties (Lev 20:10; Deut 22:22). This only changed when Rome removed from the Jews the right of capital punishment. Then adultery required divorce, not as an option as until recent times it was deemed a ground to sue for divorce, but as mandatory. If adultery has taken place, the marriage must end, because effectively the act of adultery broke it.

Emperor Augustus in the *Lex Iulia* of 18 BCE reaffirmed this requirement in Roman law by promulgating laws that indeed made it possible to prosecute men who failed to follow through on this mandatory requirement. When Matthew repeats Jesus' strict stance on divorce as itself forbidden (Matt 5:31–32; 9:9), he adds what would always have been assumed as an exception, namely this requirement that where adultery had taken place the marriage must end.

Why Marriage Mattered

All this meant that marriage, too, was taken very seriously. Unlike today, it could never be seen as simply a choice between two individuals. It was a matter for the whole family, indeed the extended family since their welfare depended on it. It was not to be left to whim or the romantic attachments that might form between young men and young women. Indeed, dating among such was seriously frowned upon and mostly forbidden, not least because it could bring disaster upon the family with, for instance, unwanted pregnancies.

Marriage was a matter for negotiation between the heads of families, namely the fathers. It was their role to seek a suitable match for their offspring. It might include identifying who might be compatible and even who might have affection for one another, but primarily it was a matter of who might make the best team to manage the household's future.

This had further implications. Normally men needed to be sufficiently established to have a household. The widespread norm, often explicitly stated, was the man should be around thirty, not by chance the age at which Jesus took the unusual step of not marrying but embarking on his ministry (Luke 3:23). For the expectation was that all men should marry. With women the age was usually very young, indeed, as soon after they begin menstruating as feasible, to avoid dangers of pregnancy out of wedlock.

Virginity mattered for them especially because it gave some indication that the woman would be likely to remain chaste during marriage and not create the chaos of engaging in adulterous liaisons. Thus, men valued virginity highly.

How Men Viewed Women

The usually large disparity between the age of the man, around thirty, and the age of the woman at marriage, often half his age, had further consequences. Wise counsel to men was that they should treat their young wives both as lovers and as daughters whom they should educate in the ways of household management. Based on the fact that their wives were much younger, less mature and experienced, men quite naturally reached the conclusion that women were by nature less mature and inferior to men. It seemed to make sense of their experience, even though we recognize it as a fallacy.

The consequences of this fallacy for women were clear. Normally men should be the heads of families and should manage the important matters beyond the household. Normally men should be the ones to take part in public discourse. They would not have understood this as misogyny, since, at least, at best, they saw their wives as also God's creation and valued partners, even though by nature not their equals.

Inevitably such views found their underpinning in religious and philosophical tradition. Thus, Plato sees women coming into being as the result of what happened when some men failed. They became women, a lower life form, in their next life. Plato develops a theory of devolution. From men at the top, a scale of lowliness develops through progressive failures that end with abject failure represented in the worms that hug the ground.

The Jewish tradition also sees woman as derived from man (Gen 2:18–23), but not as something negative. It was rather God's choice and seen as something good. In the Greek translation of these originally Hebrew texts it was possible, however, to read a stronger sense of the inequality. The Hebrew word *adam*, meaning a human being, was difficult to translate consistently into Greek and as the creation story goes on becomes the name, Adam, which in turn tells the listener that God originally created a male, Adam, not just a human being.

As in the Hebrew, the man, now seen as Adam the male, was created in the image of God (Gen 1:26–27), but when the Greek comes to speak of God's intent to create a companion for him (Gen 2:18), the translators repeat the phrase "Let us make . . . " from Gen 1:26 here too, instead of "I shall make . . . " as in the Hebrew of Gen 2:18. And in Gen 2:20 where the Hebrew reports that after the creation of the animals there was still "not found a helper as his partner," the Greek reads "not found a helper *like* him." The reference to likeness, not in the Hebrew, echoes the statement in Gen 1:26 about the man being made in the likeness of God.

The effect is to link the creation of the man and the creation of the woman closely together as reflecting the same process. Accordingly, the man was made in the image of God and the woman was made in the image of the man, one step inferior in the order of being. Paul read it this way (1 Cor 11:3, 7), though with a touch of humor he also reminded men that while woman was made from man, they all as men were made through women (11:12)!

Norms and Exceptions

There is so much that flows from an understanding of the context of what we find in the New Testament about women and about sexuality. It explains why the twelve apostles Jesus chose were male, why Paul instructed that women should remain silent in church gatherings and wait till they are home to talk with their husbands about what went on (1 Cor 14:33–36), and why they should retain their veiled hair while in church gatherings and not discard it (11:2–16).

It also explains why, as Christian communities sought to defend their respectability, they embraced their own version of what were common household codes, which instructed wives to obey their husbands, children their parents, and slaves their masters (Col 3:18—4:1; Eph 5:216:9, and imposed even more restrictions on women (1 Tim 2:8–15).

These were the norms of their day. Yet despite these norms there were exceptions. In the apocrypha we read of Judith, who as a widow managed her husband's estate and engaged in a daring assassination of her nation's enemy before then returning to her household role. It was probably a story meant to help boost support for Queen Salome Alexandra, who as King Alexander Janneus's widow succeeded him. Jewish tradition also knew of Jewish female prophets.

In the traditions about Jesus we also see exceptions. Matthew highlights women in his genealogy of Jesus (1:1–18), constructed along usual male lines of succession, but dotted with four instances of women, Tamar, Rahab, Ruth, and the unnamed wife of Uriah the Hittite, but for the last, all of them clearly gentile, all of them engaging in sexually unorthodox behavior and all of them nevertheless seen by Jews as heroes, indeed, Tamar, Rahab and Ruth, later as proselytes. Matthew wants Mary to be seen in the same light, not as having done similarly, but as the subject of allegations of having done so. These women also symbolize the inclusion of outsiders, as women and as gentiles, in God's favor, as do the gentile magi who come to honor the baby Jesus.

Matthew is following an emphasis that goes back to the beginning where women are often contrasted with men as those who hear and understand the message of Jesus whereas men do not (Mark 14:3–9; Luke 7:36–50; John 4:42). Their support for Jesus' ministry (Luke 8:1–3; Mark 15:40–41), but especially their presence in the Easter stories (Mark 16:1–8) highlights this reversal of values. Not the proud males but the women of Israel and also the marginalized, the poor and the sinners, the Samaritans and the gentiles, acclaim Jesus. At the bottom of the social heap there is often a sense of all struggling equally together. As the movement climbed socially, other norms asserted themselves.

More significantly, Jesus appears to have confronted men about the way they handle their sexuality, including in the saying with which we began. His warnings that follow this saying lay it on the line with hyperbole. Pluck out your eye, cut off your hand or your feet, if that is what it takes not to engage in sexual predation (5:29–30). Calling men to account for their sexual behavior placed responsibility where it belonged instead of blaming women or seeing them as the danger. This would have made it much easier for women to be part of the discipleship group and join the itinerants.

Women in Leadership

While males dominated the leadership, as one would expect given the social context, we also find significant exceptions, not least in the early days of the movement where Paul, in greeting fellow workers in his letter to the Romans, lists women among his fellow workers, Prisca, Mary, Junia ("prominent among the apostles" 16:7), and Tryphaena and Tryphosa (16:3–12), and in 1 Corinthians 11 reflects that he affirms that some women would exercise leadership in praise and prophecy in communal gatherings.

The valuing of all, male and female, slave and free, Jew and gentile, in Christ, as Paul puts it (Gal 3:28), had the potential to subvert all forms of discrimination. The Roman, Seneca, could affirm that slaves should also be seen as human beings worthy of dignity, but such views rarely had significant social consequences. In Paul we see some progress, but it is far from complete.

Being one in Christ did not on his understanding mean that people ceased to be male and female, slave and free, Jew and gentile. He did not advocate that slaves should be set free or should seek their freedom (1 Cor 7:21–24). Jews remained Jews and gentiles remained gentiles. Men remained men, made in the image of God, and women remained women, made in the image of men according to his reading of his Scriptures in Greek. While he could affirm that in Christ both are loved by God, this did not lead him further to undo the structural inequality embedded in the social system of his day.

His later admirers sought to rationalize the status quo, rationalizing it with reference to Eve having been the first to sin:

> Let a woman learn in silence with full submission. 12I permit no woman to teach or to have authority over a man; she is to keep silent. 13For Adam was formed first, then Eve; 14and Adam was not deceived, but the woman was deceived and became a transgressor. 15Yet she will have security through childbearing, provided they continue in faith and love and holiness, with modesty.* (1 Tim 2:11–15)

I modify the NRSV translation to replace "be saved" by "have security" because it makes better sense of the allusion to Gen 3:16 according to which women's hope will lie in the security of being subject to their husbands and their constant returning to their husbands and bearing children under their husbands' protection.

Such provisions certainly ruled out women assuming leadership in the church, although exceptions persisted. As those who managed households, they would surely have had a major role in providing infrastructure support for the house churches, the normal form of church life in the first centuries, so that it is no surprise that 2 John actually addresses such a group in association with the woman who heads it.

Where we no longer agree with the fallacious male assumption about women's inferiority and the conclusions that flowed from it, we have to revisit all such limitations. They persist still in our society, even in churches where we have long since seen that ordaining women to leadership is entirely appropriate. In that sense the Bible certainly does not tell it all in relation to family and sexuality. Its writers were as limited in their perceptions as we should expect, just as they had limited understandings of human reproduction let alone the origin and age of the universe. To take them seriously is to respect that.

Celibacy

In his exchange with the Corinthians Paul had to counter some extreme positions. One was partly a result of his own preferences. Either summarizing his own view or citing what Corinthians saw as his view, Paul declares: "It is good for man not to touch a woman" (1 Cor 7:1), a reference to sexual engagement, but then goes on to affirm marriage, indeed to defend it. Clearly Paul did not mean that sex was sinful.

Instead, he was dealing with a serious misunderstanding that had arisen among some in Corinth according to which all believers should be celibate, that is, refrain from engaging in sexual intercourse, including those who were married. They were apparently advocating the view that all people should live in the present the way they will in the future age (7:2–7).

It is not too difficult to see how the misunderstanding arose. For Mark attributes to Jesus the view that the age to come would be without sex.

> When they rise from the dead, they neither marry nor are given in marriage, but are like angels in heaven. (12:25)

There was, indeed, a minority of Jewish authors who imagined the heavenly world as a temple. That carried with it the implication that sex and sexual relations would have no place there. The widespread rule across most ancient cultures of the region was that any emission of fluid, whether in sexual intercourse or in menstruation or childbirth, rendered people inadmissible into holy spaces like temples. They would have first to undergo ritual cleansing before they would be permitted to enter. This meant that there should never be sexual activity in holy places.

It never usually implied anything negative about sex or marriage. It was simply a matter of there being an appropriate time and place and that was not in a sanctuary. One view held by some Jews was that the garden of Eden was a sanctuary and that the future paradise will be so as well. Jesus and the Jesus movement seem to have adopted this view.

We see this view also in the book of Revelation. Revelation 7 speaks in highly symbolic language of a two-stage entry into the heavenly world. First the 144,000, then "a great multitude that no one could count, from every nation, from all tribes and peoples and language" (7:9). In Revelation 14 the author describes the 144,000 as those "who have not defiled themselves with women, for they are virgins" (14:3–4). The author is using "defiled" in its ritual or cultic sense, not a moral sense and certainly not to suggest women are dirty nor to imply that marriage and sexuality are sinful, but it does refer to people who were celibate.

Paul reflects similar assumptions when he writes of couples who may want to abstain from sexual intercourse for the sake of prayer (1 Cor 7:5), by implication because they were thereby entering holy space. His advice is, however, that this should be temporary, and that they should afterwards return to full sexual engagement. His own preference for celibacy, which he sees as a calling, also makes sense in the light of these assumptions. He believed he was living in the last days. Soon he would enter holy time and space. What is the point in his or anyone else marrying?

Yet Paul did not agree with those at Corinth who wanted to make celibacy an obligation on all and believed all should live now as they will then. Throughout 1 Corinthians 7 he resists this view strongly. While he saw it as making more sense to remain celibate, given the shortness of time and nature of the age to come, he affirmed marriage for those who felt they wanted and needed to go ahead with their strong feelings for each other. Having sex without being married was, of course, out of the question. Marrying was the appropriate option and to marry was not, he emphasized, to sin or to be unworthy (7:8–9, 28, 36).

It appears that in Matthew's community there may have been similar movements, because he has Jesus address the fact that some, including himself and John the Baptist, were called to celibacy, for which he uses the image of being voluntary eunuchs, not a category usually deemed respectable, but typical of Jesus to choose such imagery (19:10–12). The point that Matthew is having Jesus make is that the calling to be celibate is not for everyone and certainly not something to be imposed on others.

It was, however, not too long before we find in early Christianity the inevitable emergence of the notion that those who live as they will do so in the age to come, namely celibate people, have a higher holiness. This was reinforced by the doubtful wisdom of Greek and Roman popular philosophies that denigrated human passions and even promoted abandoning marriage and sexual intercourse. A reading of Jesus' saying along the lines of the one apologized for at the head of this chapter reinforced such views. To engage in sexual behavior made you a second-class Christian. The purest woman was a virgin like Mary or Anna, who when widowed remained unmarried (Luke 2:36–37). So many concluded that sex must be somehow bad.

Divorce

Originally unrelated to adultery in Jewish law, which required the death penalty for adultery, divorce became mandatory when executions were forbidden. Aside from that exception, the evidence suggests that Jesus took a strict line against the practice of divorce and, of course, saw any remarriage after divorce as adultery, since the divorce was invalid in the first place (Mark 10:2–12).

Divorce was not so necessary as long as the practice persisted of allowing polygyny, namely having more than one wife. This permitted a husband not to expel the wife with whom he was no longer happy but simply to add another, with stories then of men falling in love again with their first wife. Once the option of polygyny was removed or deemed no longer respectable, as it certainly was not in Greek and Roman society, divorce became the main instrument for dealing with marital dissatisfaction.

This, in turn, opened the possibility that men might divorce wives for quite trivial reasons such as bad cooking. Jewish tradition preserves disputes on such matters between the ancient school of Shammai and Hillel before the time of Jesus. It is, in that sense, not surprising that the matter came before Jesus for comment and his response is clear (Mark 10:2–9). He affirms that divorce was never meant to be. People were meant to become one flesh and never part. He cited Genesis 1:27 and 2:24. There are independent sayings attributed to him that make the same point (Mark 10:10–12; Luke 16;18; Matt 5:31–32; 9:9; 1 Cor 7:10–12).

Read as statements of unchangeable law these closed the door on divorce and have left those who see it this way with little choice but to try to work their way around it by dubious means, such as trying to show that a marriage was not real or legitimate in the first place. Many churches have however come to see a better way forward. This is to take seriously Jesus' own stance in relation to biblical laws, namely of giving priority to the law of love and compassion for human need over commandments that might conflict with this. In many instances, most clearly in cases of domestic abuse, the most caring way forward is to allow divorce (and so remarriage) and this can apply also to a range of situations that have led to the break-down of marriages.

The matter of marriage and divorce is not to be taken lightly, but in all, informed compassion needs to determine the way ahead. Sometimes marriage relationships do break down. Already Paul pointed in this direction. In the very same chapter in which he cited Jesus' prohibition of divorce he acknowledged reluctantly just a few verses later that in circumstances where coming to faith created a marriage crisis, divorce was to be treated as a way forward (1 Cor 7:12–16). In Jewish law, which, of course, Paul assumes, divorce entailed giving the partner a certificate that freed them to marry again.

The early church also modelled this flexible non-legalistic approach when it rejected the insistence of the fundamentalist believers in the church that all gentile men must be circumcised because the Bible clearly said so in Genesis 17. The church in its wisdom determined that the more compassionate way forward was to override that requirement, as we noted in the chapter above on the law.

Same-Sex Relations

Issues of marriage and sexuality are often intimate and personal and controversies over them usually raise emotions. They are, after all, dealing with core elements of our existence as human beings. This has been evident in recent discussions of homosexuality.

The common assumption among Jews, including those who joined the Jesus movement, and whose views have survived, is that all people are heterosexual. The Genesis creation story states that God made male and female (1:27) and they took that as excluding any other variant. They were aware that in Greek and Roman culture some people saw this very differently. It is not true, as one sometimes hears people claim, that the ancient world was unaware of claims that some people are homosexual.

Plato, for instance, in his dialogue called the *Symposium*, has one of his fictional characters, Aristophanes, put up a theory to support the naturalness of both heterosexual and homosexual desire. According to the myth, human beings were once male, female, and androgynous (both male and female at the same time). They offended Zeus by behaving arrogantly, so Zeus sliced them in half. Ever since the two halves have been wanting to re-join: males with males, females with females, and males with females and vice versa.

It is not Plato's view, who writes against it, but it reflects that the notion was around at the time that some people are naturally gay. Philo of Alexandria, the Jewish teacher and philosopher who was well versed in the literature of the surrounding cultures, knows and cites the myth, only to reject it outright as contradicting what, he asserts, every Jew knew who had been brought up to respect the law of Moses. For God created only male and female.

Jews saw themselves as upholding God's law and viewed many of the practices of their pagan world as abhorrent. In the arena of same-sex attraction Philo is typical in pointing to a wide range of abuses, especially of minors and slaves, and highlighting as typical the outrageous behavior that often took place at parties where, fueled by alcohol, men engaged promiscuously with both women and men. The range of behaviors included also adult to adult consensual male intercourse as well as female to female, the latter as something less often addressed, but usually with much wider disapproval. Pedophilia may well be the original target of Jesus' dramatic warning that it would be better to be thrown into the seas with a millstone around your neck than to lead little children astray (Mark 9:42).

There were laws in Rome against citizens engaging in such acts with fellow citizens, though not with inferiors such as slaves and non-citizens. There were also stories of such behavior taking place in the imperial household of Caligula and Nero.

Paul On Same-Sex Relations

When Paul writes to Romans in preparation for his visit to communities there, which owed their foundation to others, he is concerned to counter what he knew was the bad press some had been giving him in Rome. The bad press resulted from his conflicts with leading apostles over interpretation of Scripture. He begins, therefore, by seeking to establish common ground. He does this partly by citing a statement about the core of the faith that he knew they would share (1:3–5).

When he moves beyond his initial greeting and embarks upon his attempt to account for his gospel, he begins by depicting the depravity of the pagan world (1:18–23). He knew that this, too, was common ground and would win their assent. He chooses to highlight that depravity by writing about what he portrays as a perversion of God's creation, namely men and women being sexually attracted to those of their own sex (1:24–28).

He relates this to their failure to acknowledge God rightly and suggests that this perverted understanding of God leads to their being perverted in themselves, which as a result produces in them desires that are contrary to nature, that is, how God created people to be. His focus is not primarily pederasty and other such abuses, but more broadly on people having such feelings, including in adult to adult mutual liaisons, where they burn with passion for one another (1:27). Such a state of being, he argues, is symptomatic of their sinful corruption. He may have been aware of reports of abuses in Rome's imperial household, but his concern is wider than that.

He also includes women having such feelings. Some have suggested his concern there may be with other matters such as different ways of having intercourse, like anal or oral sex or sex with animals, but the context suggests that he, like Philo, is targeting women on the same issue as men, same-sex relations. As a Jew he knew the prohibition of same-sex relations between men, or at least of men taking the role of someone's wife in such encounters, as an abomination (Lev 18:22; 20:13). Jews before him had broadened this to apply to all such encounters between men and between women and he appears to do the same. Elsewhere Paul does no more than list "male-bedders" (the literal meaning of the word he uses) and effeminates, probably alluding to the partners in same-sex relations (1 Cor 6:9), as does his imitator in 1 Timothy 1:9–10.

Nothing suggests his concern in Romans 1 is limited only to certain circumstances, such as behavior in pagan temples, or in male prostitute brothels, or in other pederastic practices or is limited only to acts and the intent to act, as some have suggested, and not the desire itself. For Paul it is something much more fundamental: people's state of being. Their distorted stance towards God has rendered them distorted. This is typical of Paul's approach to understanding the human condition, which never stops just at acts and attitudes, but always addresses people's state of being. Unlike elsewhere, he depicts this state of being as a consequence not of Adam's sin, but of the individual's failure to acknowledge God. They have minds that produce perverted desires, as he sees it.

Paul is far from seeking to be controversial. Rather, he is stating views that he knew his hearers in Rome would affirm. In just a few verses, Paul presents a strong argument. It is based on his and their presupposition that all people are heterosexual. Accordingly, anyone who might claim to be homosexual is in reality in an unnatural state of being as a result of sin, contrary to nature, contrary to how God created human beings to be.

For today's fundamentalists from right or left who find it hard to cope with acknowledging that the Bible says anything that contradicts their views or that does not fit with reality, such a reading of the plain sense of the text creates a high level of anxiety. There have been all kinds of attempts to explain away what Paul said, to make it acceptable.

Given however Paul's starting point, his conclusions are clear and plausible. The implications, then, are that we need to offer such people healing and help to be restored to their heterosexual self. There have been many attempts to follow this through, often with great patience and endurance, providing opportunities for reversion therapy, a practice now widely discredited and disallowed.

Same-Sex Relations Reassessed

If, however, we come to conclude that Paul's assumption that all people are naturally heterosexual does not tell it all, but that some people appear to be genuinely and naturally gay, then it is not appropriate, indeed it is irresponsible, to apply what Paul says to their situation. This has been the wisdom that has led many legislatures to legalize gay marriage and has led many churches to embrace gay people with the same love and respect and responsibility as heterosexual people. In his approach to the issue of circumcision and food laws Paul models an approach of how also to engage his own statements in these few verses in Romans.

The most persuasive argument leading to this realization about the fallibility of Paul's assumptions has not been academic but personal. There are simply too many good people who are gay and clearly not in a state of being to be described as sin. What is more some of them have been or are leading figures in modern societies.

In addition, many families have had the experience of seeing that one of their children is naturally gay, including families where such awareness has been very painful to acknowledge because they have a strongly conservative or fundamentalist faith. Among them I have found desperate attempts to resolve their problem, including, for instance, by misconstruing Paul as concerned only with homosexual acts and the desire to perform them.

Again, this is about acknowledging that the Bible does not tell it all on these matters any more than it did on matters of women and divorce. To take the Bible seriously means to hear what its authors were saying in their context and why they were saying it and then to draw implications for what we now must do in the light of what we might have learned in the meantime.

Much which the Bible promotes on matters of marriage and sexuality remains, nonetheless, fundamental for faith today, not least the affirmation of marriage both for reproduction and for intimate companionship.

Reflection: What does it mean to take issues of sexuality and gender seriously today?

Afterword:
From Fundamentalism to Fundamentals

No one is born a fundamentalist, though some are born into fundamentalist contexts. Nothing in my family predisposed me to the fundamentalist path. It simply made sense given what I encountered as a boy in my church. Even there the label "fundamentalist" would not have been fitting. The fervent teacher who challenged me as a ten-year-old to "make a decision" and follow Jesus did not fit that category, or not quite.

This ten-year-old did embark, however, on a journey that led him to assume and acquire what one would call fundamentalist views. Call it a naïve fundamentalism, it was an approach to Scripture that saw it as infallible. It was God's Word, a timeless source of inspiration and instruction. Young men from the New Zealand Bible Training Institute, who took up placements in our local church, helped turn what was a naïve and unquestioned approach into an ideology.

My thinking and inquiring mind wanted to know more in order to benefit from reading God's Word and to defend it. At age eleven I counted it an honor to read Psalm 46 at the church anniversary. The principal of the school I attended was present and I am guessing this in part prompted his decision to appoint me at age twelve the head boy prefect of the school. That role included raising the New Zealand flag at special assemblies, but also giving speeches, including, as I remember, parts of a speech given by King George V of England.

My minister, a jovial Cornishman, employed half as hospital chaplain and half as our minister, and far from being a fundamentalist, took a great interest in young people. He gave me books to read but went further. He had me take my first service at age thirteen. At age fourteen I received a desk calendar holder from him, and it still sits on my desk, having had sixty-two refills.

It was about this time that I set myself the task of reading four chapters of the Bible a day and underlining what I saw as significant verses. I can remember at age twelve debating with a Mormon school friend about what "I and the Father are one" (John 10:30) probably meant in its context in John's Gospel and arguing that one could not simply replace "are one" by an equals sign (= one). At age thirteen I wrote an essay seeking to understand the Trinity. The son of the concerned Presbyterian minister down the road fed me 1 John 5:8 as a key text in case I should go astray in my thinking, unaware, as I later discovered, that it was a late interpolation into the text.

I was beginning to acquire a wide knowledge of the Bible and to learn some of its key texts off by heart. There were organizations that specialized in printing such key texts on individual cards, such as the Navigators. They could then be put together in a sequence to be used in evangelism. The Billy Graham Crusade, which visited Auckland in 1959, did the same. I was trained as a counselor, at age fifteen the youngest, and so learned the sequence that declares that all have sinned and fallen short of the glory of God (Rom 3:23); the wages of sin is death but the gift of God is eternal life (Rom 6:23); but that "God so love the world that he gave his only begotten Son that whosoever believeth in him should not perish but have everlasting life" (John 3:16), always in the 1611 Authorized Version of King James, whose quaint English was somehow also suggestively divine.

It puzzled me that so many people, including my minister and many others in the church, failed to see the obvious. All have sinned and so all will go to hell. Jesus came to save people from their sins. If they believe in him, they will be saved and will not go to hell. Why was that not clear? Why did people not preach this? Why did people not seem to care that most people were going to hell? Wasn't it an ongoing emergency that required those who have been saved and born again to be out there trying to save others?

It made sense to hear visiting evangelists talk of their great pain and distress as they contemplated people writhing in the lake of fire. I joined these evangelists' pain. Such concern informed my engagement in teaching and preaching, whether in leading children's groups in the church's education program, doing "devotions" at the local youth group, or taking services. I sometimes found it odd that my minister seemed almost to want to discourage me from being so straightforward about what people needed to be told. I put it down to the devil undermining the gospel.

Teenage Years

As I moved through my teenage years, I joined up with Auckland's Youth for Christ, which fed my faith. I soon served with them as a teenage evangelist, running missions and speaking at large rallies and in the open air. I now reflect that those who afforded me such opportunities to save the world were sometimes very daring because, while they hailed my maturity and seeming wisdom, I was still just a teenager who had much to learn.

Despite having some misgivings and recognizing that I was still growing up, my minister kept giving me opportunities and this included putting me in charge of the church library, something I was to build up from the start. I set about giving the books plastic covers and exploring the books themselves. He said to me that if there were any books that I would like to keep, I should do so.

I was fascinated to find among the donations a set of John Wesley's sermons, an eighteenth-century edition, where many of the "s"s are printed as "f"s. I had no idea of their value, but fortunately my reading and underlining (!) there, too, reached only as far as the first sermon on salvation by faith.

Since my Bible in which I immersed myself was already in the old English of 1611, to read the eighteenth-century English of John Wesley proved no hurdle. It was probably one of the most influential experiences of my youth. It didn't challenge my fundamentalism. It didn't address the Bible in that sense, but it made a strong case for what is at its center, put in the non-inclusive language of the day: all men need to be saved; all men can be saved; all men can know they are saved; all men can be saved to the uttermost.

I was largely unaware of the novelty of these statements designed to counter popular views that only some are destined to be saved. The impact for me was on the centrality of love for all and that this not only saved them but that there were to be consequences already in this life, something John Wesley described as sanctification. I could embrace what he said because it fitted well with my version of the gospel, but it enriched it with the notion of love as universal and being saved as more than just going to heaven and not to hell.

I pressed the logic of my faith also in other directions. A further obvious truth that people seemed reluctant to believe and act upon was prayer. "Prayer changes things" was a slogan I took to heart. If enough people pray hard enough, God will change things. Surely, if we really care about people, we should become prayer warriors. Every hour spent in prayer would change the world. Why did people not take this seriously? Why were only a few of us rising early in the morning to plead with God to do things? People were sick. People were hungry. People were sinning. People were rushing along the broad way that leads to destruction and hell. Surely the answer was obvious. Pray more!

Questioning

Already by my late teenage years I was beginning to refine my thinking in this area. It seemed to me clear at the time, at least from what I was told and believed, that people were being miraculously healed in answer to prayer, but that others were not. The standard answer: God answers prayer but not always as you expect and one day what seems like a tangle of threads when you look at the wrong side of an embroidered bookmark will be seen as a perfect design when you turn it round the right way. Motor accidents? Famines? Really? I didn't know of the Holocaust at that stage.

Perhaps unconsciously my openness to believe that God does not destine people to hell, also encouraged me to believe that God is present in our world in different ways. Despite the miracles of the stilling of the storm and Jesus' walking on water, I reached the conclusion that God does not arrange and change the weather in answer to prayer, or plan that people get cancer or have motor accidents, let alone die of starvation. I began to conclude that it made best sense to understand God as changing people or at least as moving in people not things. Even then people can resist God. So my praying became more along the lines of prayer that God would move in people's lives, prompt and speak to them. This seemed to make better sense of what I was observing around me.

Despite what I and others would have claimed, in the mix that was my fundamentalism, there were elements that had no basis in the Bible. My fundamentalism did not go so far as banning going to movies or playing cards, but it certainly included banning smoking, drinking alcohol, even dancing. My exposure, however, to people who I thought had a sound faith and, in my judgment, displayed the fruits of the Spirit disturbed some of these and other assumptions.

There really were "Spirit-filled" Christians, as I would have put it, who drank wine and beer, smoked and danced. Some nuns, it struck me, were also "Spirit-filled" believers, even though they were Catholic! How could this be? The language of being "Spirit-filled" came into my vocabulary especially through mixing with Youth for Christ friends, some of whom belonged to Pentecostal churches. I was also aware that there was an underlying tension in the movement between these and others.

The combination of that influence and the impact of John Wesley's teaching on sanctification, led me to self-examination as part of my Christian life. I needed to monitor constantly if I was right with God and for this another "memory verse" helped: "If we confess our sins, he is faithful and just to forgive us our sins and to cleanse us from all unrighteousness" (1 John 1:9). Did I have the joy of the Spirit? If not, what did I need to confess? Being saved was one thing. Walking in the Spirit was another.

The move to develop a spiritual awareness also changed some of my perspectives. In fact it shifted the center of my faith to what I described as my ongoing relationship with God and also enabled me to read Scripture in a new light and not through the narrow prism of what it might say about evangelism and who would and would not be saved.

It also created some problems. When I had a cold, I did not seem to have the joy of the Spirit and certainly not if I had a headache, though that was rare. I learned that feelings matter but that feelings vary. Faith was not about looking for mountaintop experiences or highs. That sounded a little too much like drug addiction. John Wesley's third affirmation then proved a wise compromise. We can know we are right with God, if we are open before ourselves and before God, whether our feelings are on a high or not. Our assurance of love is not the feeling, which one may want to hype up through hyperventilation (a much later insight), but the person of God. God's love is bigger and more reliable than my feelings.

Finding Fundamentals

Already this was a beginning of moving from fundamentalism to fundamentals. One of those fundamentals is that God is good, and God is loving. I was far from having any doubts about God's right then to condemn unbelievers to eternal punishment. That was still intact, but my faith in God as good and loving did affirm and reinforce my father's encouragement to me as a little boy, never to be afraid to ask questions.

I am aware that I am using the word, "fundamentals," in a different sense from when it was used at the beginnings of fundamentalism, where it functioned defensively to protect doctrines such as the inerrancy of the Bible. I am using "fundamentals" to refer to what I see as core values for my faith as articulated in this book.

For many years I was very critical of theological education because it seemed to render people hopelessly out of touch with what to me made sense for a life of faith. Nevertheless, and partly in order change that situation, I took steps to apply to become a candidate for ministry. They would not destroy my faith. I would help to change things for the better. I knew what the gospel was, and I had an extensive knowledge of the Bible, much greater than most of my peers.

I admire the patience of the principal of the theological college when I declared to him that God did not want me to go to university. "That's not God, that's you," he replied. I reluctantly submitted and agreed to commence the first year of a Bachelor of Arts degree, which I could complete while doing my ministerial studies over the following three years. Somehow, I was able to entertain that he was right, perhaps because I could see that my faith and competence would certainly be enriched by carrying on what I had already initiated, namely learning Greek. Despite my love of the King James version, which I could hold aloft in devotion in its Thompson Chain Reference shiny floppy black leather, I knew that the original was Hebrew and Greek.

It was also time to move beyond self-education. I had spent my first year after completing school, at age 18, initially as a builder's laborer working on the construction of a supermarket. From digging its foundations to sweeping it clean on the day of its opening, it provided a rich learning experience. Those four months were followed by working just three days a week at a grocery warehouse, which enabled me to run a weekly children's Happy Hour, an after school evangelistic event, and to do youth work for the local church.

At 17 in my final year of school I had run the Crusaders Club, a weekly lunchtime gathering of students with a speaker or a film, designed to spread the faith across the school, sometimes drawing over 100 students. That year and the following years I was deeply involved in children's camp experiences, teaching in the local church, where I adapted John Wesley's sermon as study material for the youth group, and preaching in my church and as a teenage evangelist.

Crusaders was related to the Evangelical Union, its equivalent in the university, and, when I commenced university, aged 19, I was a keen attender. Once we had the great conservative New Testament scholar, Professor F. F. Bruce, address us. His message was clear. Be informed about your faith. He meant, in particular, study the classics and world of the New Testament and not just its language.

This was so affirming. I was embarking upon a degree that included two years of Latin, building upon the five years I had had at school, three years of Greek, two years of Hebrew, one of English and one of German, an exceptional combination that my classics professor ensured was approved on the basis that the balance of broader study would come through my study in the theological college.

Studying Theology

My first year at the theological college, when I was just 20 years old, opened me to a range of issues of which I had little awareness or had known only as mediated through my conservative and fundamentalist circles and such media as the "Herald of his Coming" and the Ecuador-based radio station, "Heralding Christ Jesus' Blessings." But I knew my Bible, and this not only had helped me to achieve highly in Youth for Christ quizzes, but also to make connections when introduced to the serious study of the Bible.

I was confident that God was beside me and encouraging me to explore, to be open, to be critical, and through it all to hold to what had become the fundamentals of my faith. In my first Old Testament assignment I sought to prove that Moses wrote the Pentateuch, the first five books of the Bible. Later I produced an assignment to prove that Paul wrote the Pastoral Epistles, 1 and 2 Timothy and Titus. I was given a fail for neither, but, on the contrary, encouraged to keep exploring. Brilliant educators!

My theological and historical explorations were going on at the same time as my Greek and Latin studies at the university were introducing me not just to the language but also to the world that spoke Latin and Greek, the world, indeed, of the New Testament. It was as though in my personal life, history was repeating itself. For the major advances in New Testament scholarship began to emerge in the eighteenth century, in particular, as scholars made connections not just between the language of the New

Testament and its linguistic world, but also between that world and the thought world of the New Testament.

It soon became clear to me, as it did in the eighteenth and nineteenth century, that the Old Testament and the New Testament were different in many respects, that they were not composed at one point of time by God or by a godly few, but reflected up to seven or eight hundred years of writing, and that the New Testament itself comprised books by different authors over a fifty-year period beginning some fifteen to twenty years after Jesus. What was once a timeless authoritative text, suddenly became a complex and diverse collection, not because modern scholars said so, but because it was so. You just needed to read it more carefully. The two-dimensional had become the three-dimensional.

The Bible Coming Alive

This was exciting. I was very aware that some used such knowledge to discredit the Bible. These were the days when some were claiming God is dead, or claiming that we cannot get back to the historical Jesus and that to try to do so was to fail to see that faith must be in the living Christ, the Word, and could never be subject to the ambiguities and uncertainties of historical reconstruction. Skepticism became almost an article of faith for some in order to focus on what they held as their fundamentals.

I was on the other side and could never embrace such skepticism, ideological or otherwise. The new conservative scholars like F. F. Bruce portrayed historical awareness and exploration as a way to enhance our understanding of the New Testament and its significance and that certainly worked for me. I was reading not a timeless book but a collection of witnesses to faith in real situations. This was faith coming to life. I could recognize and be inspired by what I read in a different way.

In many ways my first year in theological college was overwhelming and I had other lessons to learn. One was that it is simply too much to take a full-time load of degree studies, and a full-time year of theological education and spend my weekends engaged in all my favorite outreach activities. The exhaustion brought me down to my knees and thankfully I had the support to recover myself and learn to monitor and manage commitments and tiredness by better planning and strong discipline. It was at this time that I met my wife who supported me as I rebuilt. Her German schooling gave her what mine did not, that is, informed instruction about the New

Testament and its world. She knew something of what I was studying as most of my other friends did not.

Retracing Steps of Learning from the Nineteenth Century

A more careful reading of the Gospels produced, in the nineteenth century, some of the early attempts to explain why they had so much material in common, yet on other points differed. The Gospel according to John was a special case, expressing itself more freely in language that must have reflected the discourse of believers in its setting, language also reflected in 1 John. John's Gospel depicts Jesus' ministry as lasting three years, and that the Friday on which he died was the day before the Passover.

Any careful reading reveals that the first three Gospels have much in common and this required explanation, but also that they differed from the Fourth Gospel on matters of timing and a great deal more. They portray Jesus' ministry as lasting just one year and the Friday on which he died was Passover Day. One of my first responses to this was to seek explanations, such as that they might have been using different calendars, though that did not solve the problem of the length of Jesus' ministry.

The truth of what they, back in the nineteenth century, observed and I now learned, was not to be explained away. I did not need to tell lies about it to save my faith, because my faith was that God wanted me to trust and be open and I never needed to fear what is true. It made sense to me that in the far-flung Christian communities of believers in the Roman empire, the telling and retelling of stories would inevitably mean that such differences would arise. I am still not confident that I know whether the first three Gospels or the fourth is right on the timing, though I am inclined to support the latter.

One might cope with differences if there were just a few, but looking at the first three Gospels together, side by side, reveals that beyond their commonality there are many, many differences. Learning to read them in Greek makes that even clearer. The most widely accepted theory of how the Gospels relate, which also makes best sense to me, is that Mark's Gospel is the earliest and that Matthew and Luke both knew Mark and both had a collection of sayings, which was at least very similar if not always identical, and that each had access to materials unknown to the other.

My Greek enabled me to see that both Matthew and Luke improve Mark's Greek at times. There was however much more going on. One of my richest experiences—and I have done this more than once—has been to look at a synopsis of the Gospels, which puts the three Gospels in parallel columns enabling one then to see for oneself the similarities and differences. Color highlighters can help bring them out. In addition, it is helpful to look at the sequence of their material and see where the order is identical or has been changed.

I had been familiar with some of the explanations of why the Gospels describe the same event in different ways. One is to play the game of whispers, starting at one end of a row of people and asking them to pass on the whisper and see whether what emerged at the end of the line is the same or different from the original. Another is to observe that people looking at a mountain from different angles will see and describe it differently. These explanations crumble, however, when we look at passages like the last meal of Jesus, where what Jesus says is reported differently (Mark 14:22–25; 1 Cor 11:23–26), or like the rich man's encounter with Jesus, where it is fairly clear that Matthew has made some creative revisions to Mark's account (Mark 10:17–22; Matt 19:16–22; Luke 18:18–23).

Jesus' Encounter with the Rich Man

I have used that anecdote over the years as a simple way of observing what typically happened. In brief, Luke reproduces Mark's story with few changes. He makes the rich man a ruler, not an unreasonable assumption, and he omits one of the commandments that Mark had Jesus list, "Do not defraud," because it was not in the Ten Commandments, and he reordered the commandments to put adultery first, because that is the order in the Greek translation of the Ten Commandments.

Matthew, however, used the anecdote more creatively. He, too, omitted "Do not defraud" for the same reason, but his major innovation was to depict the rich man as a young man and see Jesus challenging him to grow up, to be mature in his faith. The word for mature also means "perfect," but Matthew is using it in the sense of grown up. He was not setting up two levels of being a believer, being an ordinary one or being a perfect one. Matthew has Jesus also add: "You shall love your neighbor as yourself." Matthew made these changes not to contradict what Mark said, though at a superficial level it does, but to bring out its point more effectively in his context.

I realized what scholars in history realized, especially as we moved into the twentieth century, that the kinds of change made by Matthew and Luke in taking up and reusing all but 30 or so verses of Mark are likely also to have been made by people before Mark. In the 30–40 year period before the Gospels were written, people would have been busy using sayings and anecdotes about Jesus, in preaching, teaching, and worship, in ever new contexts as the movement spread. What else should one expect but that there would be changes? Perhaps more notable is that so much seems to have been preserved that appears unchanged and so much of the substance, at least, of what was said remained constant.

My journey in inquiry and faith reached by now the point where I would have been simply telling lies, had I said that everything in the Gospels is historically true. No mental gymnastics were necessary. My faith meant I could be comfortable acknowledging that this was so and also acknowledging that there would be instances where I simply could not know whether something was historical or not.

I did not find and do not find attempts to avoid this reality by suggesting they learned Jesus' sayings by heart convincing, because they clearly do differ. Nor do I find convincing the suggestion the claim that there must have been someone who would have checked them for accuracy, for the same reason. Nor does the claim that every single saying preserved as said by Jesus must have been said by him on different occasions make sense to me, because there are just too many instances where only one event can be meant and where the sayings do not agree.

Why should my faith be such that I have to argue in this way? These are human witnesses to Jesus and his impact. They were not and were not seen by their authors as intricately accurate, historical reporting. The diversity is not a weakness, but a strength. At the same time, I am not skeptical of the possibilities of reproducing at least a core of the message of Jesus, despite the complex processes of transmission. As I have indicated in the chapters of this book, there is more than enough to enable us to recognize his challenges to have them inform the fundamentals for my faith.

Pastoral Theology

If the New Testament study in which I engaged excited me and liberated me from the vestiges of a fundamentalism that failed to take the Bible it revered seriously enough and read it carefully enough, my studies in pastoral theology also profoundly influenced my faith and my approach to Scripture.

The principal who confronted my declaration about university, David Williams, stood in the stream of influence that flowed through Carl Rogers and Seward Hiltner and others, and helped me to a deeper understanding of Paul, but also of my own spirituality, indeed my own self. Wholeness, integration, was a core value and was not to be achieved by imposing rules upon oneself, but by having singleness of mind. This was very biblical but could be explained in ways that also made sense of daily life.

When someone looks forward to being married, for instance, they will need to attend to many details, but that goal will have some automatic effects. It will integrate and shape all that they do, including some things that they will automatically do. Having a goal has an integrating effect. In the same way, when we set love and compassion, indeed God's love and its sharing, as our goal, then there will be some automatic shaping that will follow. It will have an integrating effect.

For me this rang bells, though the integrative effects of having a goal went only part way towards what Paul was talking about and what can really happen that brings about change. Faith is about more than having a goal. It is also about having a relationship. I had learned that setting God and God's love at the center of my life did more, especially because I saw God not as static or inactive but as active and engaging. Pastoral theology helped me understand this as well. For what Paul was writing about is what we know can be the effects of allowing oneself to be loved.

When we allow ourselves to be loved, accepted, forgiven, valued, then we can let go our guilt and our fears. We can value ourselves and stop trying to persuade ourselves and others that we merit being loved. Freed from that self-preoccupation, our energies and attention are available to be loving also towards others. Love, in this way, generates love. The more we engage in this process, the freer and more available we become. I read what Paul said about God's love, God's Spirit, producing in us the fruit of the Spirit, especially love, and it helped me make sense of why he argued that to walk in the Spirit in this way will enable you to go even beyond what the law and commandments rightly describe as good behavior.

Reading Paul now made much better sense. Walking in the Spirit, that is, connected to God and God's goal, is not primarily trying to be good or keep good commandments, but being in an integrating relationship with produces the fruits of that relationship, the fruit of the Spirit as Paul puts it.

This creates an inner dynamic that tradition going back to Jesus describes as a good tree bringing forth good fruit. This is something that all the best efforts at keeping the law cannot achieve. For the love, which is the goal, is also the love that sets us free and brings us into unity within ourselves and with God.

My earlier reflections on seeking to continue to be right with God cohered well with these insights. Now I began to acquire a better grasp of what it meant to move towards being saved to the uttermost, in Wesley's terms. I came to these insights and understanding at a time when many churches were no longer preaching a gospel focused on getting people out of hell into heaven, but were beginning to see their mission as bringing wholeness through helping people develop a relationship with God and deal with grief, guilt, and conflict through counseling and group support. This gave a corporate dimension to the gospel, which the narrower understanding of the gospel focused on individual's fate in eternity did not.

Beyond Counseling

To these fundamentals of my faith came another, partly through engaging with greater awareness of what was happening in the wider community and the wider world and partly through sensing that some forms of counseling and individual help seemed to do little more than help people live in the situations in which they found themselves, but without addressing those circumstances, themselves. While Paul wrote of sin as a power, as something that is not just about deeds, so in a modern sense we needed to see sins not just as doing deeds but as something systemic, such as structures that suppress, demean, or dominate people.

Offering a person trapped in poverty a relationship with God that brings them forgiveness, frees them from their fears, and helps their self-esteem is one thing. Addressing the evil of their context that holds them in poverty is another. My engagement in research on the historical Jesus also made it very clear to me that it makes no sense to claim to be a follower of Jesus and not to want to proclaim and be good news for the poor. As discussed in the chapter above on good news for the poor, "the poor" is not to be narrowed just to economic poverty, but it certainly includes it. It is one of the fundamentals of faith as I see it.

It had always struck me as jarring that Jesus spoke of the good news as the coming of kingdom of God, a corporate notion, whereas I had been shaped by a notion of gospel as primarily about personal salvation. It is surely both. Indeed, I remember having conversations about the preference for John's Gospel for evangelism because the other three Gospels were too liberal sounding and not evangelical enough. The other side to this story is that I was aware very early on that some had reduced the gospel to trying to establish the kingdom of God on earth, effectively in some instances reducing it to a set of ideals and oughts.

My evangelical faith, in the best sense as I understood it, insisted and insists that the gospel cannot be reduced to just an ideal or a program, but must engage people at a personal level. It must be therefore also about cultivating the tree that will bring forth fruit. Change cannot be reduced to what people might do if you lay it on them with many oughts and, sometimes, alas, with anger. Change needs to be part of what is generated by the process of enabling love and its informed expression, for which wisdom and instruction have their role to play.

Early Research Years

The research I undertook in the early years of my scholarship, now half a century in the past, focused on the diversity of models early Christians employed in claiming that in Christ God meets us in challenging and transforming ways. I embarked on a doctoral thesis in Mainz, Germany, under the guidance of Professor Ferdinand Hahn, to explore the letter to the Hebrews.

In Hebrews I could detect the ongoing impact of royal messianic hope, which had its origins in royal ideology that declared the king God's adopted son. It provided the basis for Hebrews declaring that God has enthroned Jesus at his resurrection, given him the throne name, Son of God, and crowned him Lord, a notion that Paul also preserves in writing of Jesus as having been appointed Son of God from the time of his resurrection from the dead (Rom 1:4). This stream of thought drew strongly on the royal coronation Psalms 2 and 110, especially 2:7 and 110:1.

I could also detect the very different stream of thought, which also had its origin in Jewish thought, that portrayed God's Wisdom as not just a quality but as a person, who had visited humanity seeking a place to dwell and found a place in Israel, represented by the divine law of Moses (Prov 8:22; Sir 24). In some Jewish speculation the figure is portrayed as masculine, as the Word of God. Jewish followers of Jesus then decided to apply it to Jesus, depicting Jesus as the Word having become flesh, seeking the response of faith (John 1:1–18).

Like the pessimistic Jews who claimed that no nation responded positively to wisdom (1 En. 42), John's Gospel declared that Jesus the Word, too, was rejected by his own except for those who did receive him (1:10–13). Now not the law, but Jesus alone was being described as God's Word and Wisdom and as being the image and reflection of God. This way of explaining who Jesus was went far beyond what the royal messiahship ideology provided and gave a much richer meaning to calling him Son of God.

I also came to see that these two quite different attempts to explain and expound Jesus kept company in the New Testament with a range of others, including that Jesus was miraculously conceived as the offspring of God and a woman or was an anointed prophet like Moses or Elijah. I could embrace the common theme while not sensing a need to make a choice among the explanations. The recognition of the way language functions helped me find a common underlying structure beneath the variants in expressions about Jesus and his significance, both in general, and then in my analysis of the language of the Gospel according to John.

In more recent times I have been aware, as outlined above, in the chapter on the cross, that often times, then and now, what appear to be conflicting traditions could occur side by side in a single document and that the reason that this was possible is that what holds them all together is ultimately an understanding of God. Explanations and categories used to explain the significance of Jesus not only vary but are all characterized by levels of inadequacy and this is all the more so when we seek to uses images to speak of God. When we think we have captured the meaning of God, we have probably embarked on the path of idolatry.

On Jesus' Attitude towards Biblical Law

My investigation of the way the Gospels, including some second-century gospels and traditions, portrayed Jesus' attitude towards the law enabled me to enter more fully into the world of the first believers and especially into the world of the Jewish faith in and from which they emerged. I can remember on my first full reading of the first-century Jewish teacher and philosopher, Philo of Alexandria, how impressed I was about his emphasis on God's love and mercy. The major work of Ed Sanders, challenging especially Protestant stereotypes about Jewish understanding of faith and grace, found ringing confirmation.

The discovery in 1947 of the scrolls hidden in caves at Qumran on the shores of the Dead Sea, a library of previous known works, of documents belonging to a sect, and of other previously unknown works, opened the eyes of many, including mine, to new understandings of Jewish faith in the world of Jesus and the New Testament. It did so not only by bringing these texts to light, a process that dragged on for half a century, but also because it brought about a new awareness of many of the other Jewish writings of the period and helped us to see just how much the Jesus movement is best understood as part of the mix of Judaism of the time.

My investigations of Jewish attitudes toward the biblical law, in the context of studying how the Gospels portrayed Jesus' attitude towards the law, were richly enhanced by access to this world of writings. This was even more so when I undertook major research over a five year period with a full time research professorial fellowship, 2005–2010, funded by the Australian Research Council, to investigate attitudes towards sexuality, understood in a broad sense as matters pertaining to sexuality, in early Jewish and New Testament literature, most of which was taken up with Jewish literature.

In this and other research the more I read, the more uneasy I became about what biblical scholars like myself had once believed and taught, but also about what sometimes New Testament writers, caught in the conflicts of the day with fellow Jews, had written. Some of the chapters on troubling themes in this book are the result. Much that has been written in the past about Jews and Judaism has been simply unfair and ill-informed.

I have been greatly enriched through the collegiality of international scholars, especially through the Society of New Testament Studies (*Studiorum Novi Testamenti Societas*), where since 2014 I have held responsibility for its international initiatives program, seeking to support and promote New Testament research in regions beyond the long established academies of North America and Europe. This entails working with Liaison Committees in Eastern Europe, Africa, Latin America, and the Asia Pacific. I have also been privileged to be part of the small group of leading Johannine specialists, the *Colloquium Ioanneum*, and until recently been an active participant in Jewish studies through the Enoch Seminar and the *Septuaginta Deutsch*, as well as numerous international conferences.

Within Australia I have also valued the engagement with scholars from across the disciplines as a fellow of the Australian Academy of the

Humanities where I have been section Chair of both the Religion and Classics section. I have always counted it a privilege and, indeed, also a responsibility to make New Testament scholarship widely accessible and available, whether through my writings, my online lectionary commentaries, occasional lectures, and study materials, or through leading worship, primarily within the Uniting Church in Australia as a "Minister of the Word."

Fundamentalism and Neo-Fundamentalism

For me to live and work within the Christian tradition means that I am aware both of its strength and of its weaknesses, though I do not pretend to know all about either. While I have made the journey from naïve and then ideological fundamentalism, I have also sought to resist what I call neo-fundamentalism, where people in advocating for justice and equality, in relation to gay people or women and men and much else, argue that if only people would understand Scripture they would come to agree with the position they advocate.

I encountered neo-fundamentalism regularly in reading what people have written about same-sex relations, especially in the many attempts to explain away what concerned Paul as only pederasty or only acts or intent to act, or only sex with slaves. For me, neither of these fundamentalisms, whether from right or left, makes sense. Why are people unwilling to acknowledge that there is a wide gap between current understanding of a range of matters, from human reproduction to the age of the universe, and what people believed two thousand years ago?

Why do we need to deny that and effectively lie about it? For my faith honesty and integrity is never a threat, nor is the fallibility of my understanding. To take a leaf out of Jesus' method of arguing, what parent would not want their child to explore? Do we really think God is upset if we should discover the truth or should reach different conclusions about the origin and structure of the universe from those held by the apostles and Jesus himself?

I learned very early to understand the fear that causes many on the left and right to hold to some form of fundamentalism. It is the slippery slope argument. If you begin to question, then you will be in danger of questioning everything and you will lose your faith and your salvation. I had been in that space and, while not pretending to know all the other complications that whirl around people's anxieties, my faith tells me that if to preserve my faith I need to stop asking questions, stop acknowledging life's complexities, let alone lie by arguing there are none, then my faith is not worth holding onto.

One of the strengths of taking an approach that finds a center, a core of fundamentals, especially the fundamental faith that God is loving and never ceases to be so, is that it sets me free to explore, to face the fallibility of my own conclusions and their full force when they are wrong, and follow the consequences. I do not have to have all the answers. I just need to stay on the journey and be alert and responsive. Then in the liturgies, which blend truth with aesthetics, I can celebrate a sense of companionship and belonging that seeks its ultimate fulfillment in sharing in the Creator's love and compassion in the world in which I live. Nothing is more rewarding.

As a oneness holds together the various attempts to explain the phenomenon of Jesus and what he achieved, so a oneness can hold together the various expressions of faith in a God of love and compassion, which one may find in one's own faith culture but also in that of others. That oneness will also confront what jars in one's own faith and that of others. We all walk with some grit in our shoes in religious and cultural contexts where its awareness is possible even if, by and large, its removal is not. This book is written to enhance that awareness and encourage a holding to the fundamentals that form the basis of our relationship with God and with each other.

My Published Works

Many of the issues addressed here have in part received fuller discussion in dialogue with others in already published works. These include my books on Christology (how one understands Jesus), especially in Hebrews, my doctoral thesis published in German, and in John:

Sohn und Hoherpriester. Eine traditionsgeschichtliche Untersuchung zur Christologie des Hebräerbriefes. WMANT 52. Neukirchen-Vluyn: Neukirchener Verlag, 1981, to which I returned in:
"Revisiting High Priesthood Christology in Hebrews." *Zeitschrift für die neutestamentliche Wissenschaft* 109 (2018) 235–83.
Jesus in John's Gospel: Structure and Issues in Johannine Christology. Grand Rapids: Eerdmans, 2017.

The latter two works also address questions of understanding Jesus' death, the place of the law and the attitude towards "the Jews." I have addressed the significance given to Jesus' death also in recent articles:

"Forgiveness Monopoly? Identity Formation and Demarcation in the Jesus Movement." In *Tempel, Lehrhaus, Synagoge. Orte jüdischen Gottesdienstes, Lernens und Lebens. Festschrift für Wolfgang Kraus,* edited by Christian Eberhart et al., 359–72. Paderborn: Schöningh, 2020.
"Competing Spiritualities: Reflections on John 6 in Global Perspective." In *Matthew, Paul, and Others: Asian Perspectives on New Testament Themes,* edited by William Loader et al., 275–89. Innsbruck: Innsbruck University Press. https://www.uibk.ac.at/iup/buecher/9783903187665.html. [Papers of the Society for New Testament Studies Asia Pacific Liaison Committee Conference, Taipei, 19–21 October, 2018].
"Tensions in Matthean and Johannine Soteriology Viewed in Their Jewish Context." In *Jesus and Judaism: A Contested Relationship in Context.* SBLRBS 87, edited by R. Alan Culpepper and Paul N. Anderson, 175–88. Atlanta: SBL, 2017.

My research on the law and approaches to Scripture both within Judaism and within the emerging Christian movement include:

Jesus' Attitude towards the Law: A Study of the Gospels. Grand Rapids: Eerdmans, 2002; first published as WUNT 2.97. Tübingen: Mohr Siebeck, 1997.
Jesus and the Fundamentalism of his Day. Grand Rapids: Eerdmans, 2001.
"Wisdom and Logos Traditions in Judaism and John's Christology." In *Reading the Gospel of John's Christology as Jewish Messianism: Royal, Prophetic, and Divine Messiahs,* edited by Benjamin Reynolds and Gabriele Boccaccini, 303–34. AJEC 106. Leiden: Brill, 2018.
"The Significance of the Prologue for Understanding John's Soteriology." In *The Prologue of the Gospel of John: Its Literary, Theological, and Philosophical Contexts. Papers read at the Colloquium Ioanneum 2013,* edited by Jan G. van der Watt et al., 45–55. WUNT 359. Tübingen: Mohr Siebeck, 2016.
"The Significance of 1:14–18 for Understanding John's Approach to Law and Ethics." *Review of Rabbinic Judaism* 19 (2016) 194–201.
"The Law in the New Testament." In *The Oxford Encyclopedia of the Bible and Ethics: Two-Volume Set,* edited by Robert Brawley, 1:513–18. New York/Oxford: Oxford University Press, 2014.
"Approaching the New Testament as Source of Faith and Witness to Faith." In *Hermeneutics and the Authority of Scripture,* edited by Alan H. Cadwallader, 79–96. Adelaide: Australian Theological Forum, 2011.
"Jesus and the Law." In *Handbook of the Study of the Historical Jesus,* edited by T. Holmén and S. E. Porter, 2745–72. 4 vols. Leiden: Brill, 2011.

I have discussed the issue of what became of "good news for the poor" in:

"What Happened to 'Good News for the Poor' in the Johannine Tradition?" In *John, Jesus, and History; Vol. 3, Glimpses of Jesus through the Johannine Lens,* edited by Paul N. Anderson et al., 469–80. Early Christianity and its Literature 18. Atlanta: SBL, 2016.

"What Happened to 'Good News for the Poor'? On the Trail of Hope Beyond Jesus." In *Reflections on Early Christian History and Religion*, edited by Cilliers Breytenbach and Jörg Frey, 233–66. AJEC 81. Leiden: Brill, 2012.

I have worked extensively on attitudes towards sexuality and related issues, in particular over a five-year period of full time research funded by the Australian Research Council through a professorial fellowship, 2005–2010. This includes work primarily on Jewish literature:

Enoch, Levi, and Jubilees on Sexuality: Attitudes Towards Sexuality in the Early Enoch Literature, the Aramaic Levi Document, and the Book of Jubilees. Grand Rapids: Eerdmans, 2007.
The Dead Sea Scrolls on Sexuality: Attitudes Towards Sexuality in Sectarian and Related Literature at Qumran. Grand Rapids: Eerdmans, 2009.
The Pseudepigrapha on Sexuality: Attitudes towards Sexuality in Apocalypses, Testament, Legends, Wisdom, and Related Literature. Grand Rapids: Eerdmans, 2011.
Philo, Josephus, and the Testaments on Sexuality: Attitudes towards Sexuality in the Writings of Philo, Josephus, and the Testaments of the Twelve Patriarchs. Grand Rapids: Eerdmans, 2011.
"Sexuality Issues and Conflict Development in Qumran Literature." In *"Wisdom Poured Out Like Water": Studies on Jewish and Christian Antiquity in Honor of Gabriele Boccaccini*, edited by J. Harold Ellens et al., 232–50. Deuterocanonical and Cognate Literature Studies 38. Berlin: de Gruyter, 2018.
"Sexuality in the Apocrypha." In *Oxford Handbook of the Apocrypha*, edited by Gerbern S. Oegema. Oxford: Oxford University Press, forthcoming, 2020.

Other books and articles concentrated on the connection with New Testament writings:

The New Testament on Sexuality. Grand Rapids: Eerdmans, 2012.
Making Sense of Sex: Attitudes towards Sexuality in Early Jewish and Christian Literature. Grand Rapids: Eerdmans, 2013.
"Genesis 2:24 and the Jesus Tradition." In *Jesus and the Scriptures: Problems, Passages and Patterns*, edited by Tobias Hägerland, 33–47. LNTS 552. London: T. & T. Clark, 2016.
"Marriage and Sexual Relations in the New Testament World." In *The Oxford Handbook of Theology, Sexuality, and Gender*, edited by Adrian Thatcher, 189–205. Oxford: Oxford University Press, 2015.
"'Not as the Gentiles': Sexual Issues at the Interface between Judaism and Its Greco-Roman World." *Religions* 9 (2018). http://www.mdpi.com/2077-1444/9/9/258/pdf.
"Did Adultery Mandate Divorce? A Reassessment of Jesus' Divorce Logia." *New Testament Studies* 61 (2015) 67–78.

In recent times this has included also separate discussions of the issue of same-sex relations:

"Reading Romans 1 on Homosexuality in the Light of Biblical/Jewish and Greco-Roman Perspectives of its Time." *Zeitschrift für die neutestamentliche Wissenschaft* 108 (2017) 119–49.
"Homosexuality in the New Testament." SBL *Odyssey.* http://bibleodyssey.org/en/passages/related-articles/homosexuality-in-the-new-testament.
"The Bible and Homosexuality." In *Two Views on Homosexuality, the Bible, and the Church,* edited by Preston Sprinkle, 17–48, 102–107, 148–52, 194–99. Counterpoints: Bible and Theology. Grand Rapids: Zondervan, 2016.

Many of the issues raised also come to expression in dealing with the weekly readings of the Revised Common Lectionary for which I have in recent years provided online commentary on my website: http://wwwstaff.murdoch.edu.au/~loader/, which also contains shorter discussions of some of this book's key themes. My concern has always been to share the fruits of scholarship with a wider readership. This was already the purpose of my book, *Dear Kim, This is What I Believe. Explaining the Christian Faith Today* (revised edition: http://wwwstaff.murdoch.edu.au/~loader/DearKim.htm).

I am deeply grateful for all who have joined me on the journey, sometimes singing the same song, sometimes chanting contrary melodies, and sometimes teaching me new tunes. The harmony of different voices is rich, more daring than unison, and at best inspiring and uplifting, as I seek with others to walk the path of Christian discipleship with sensitivity to its benefits and dangers.

www.ingramcontent.com/pod-product-compliance
Lightning Source LLC
Chambersburg PA
CBHW030309100426
42812CB00002B/625